Irish Children's
Writers and Illustrators
1986–2006

Irish Children's Writers and Illustrators 1986–2006

A Selection of Essays

Edited by Valerie Coghlan
and Siobhán Parkinson

Children's Books Ireland
&
Church of Ireland College of Education Publications

CICE
publications

First published by
Church of Ireland College of Education Publications
and
Children's Books Ireland
2007

The views expressed in the articles are those of the authors and do not necessarily
represent CBI or CICE publications policy.

ISBN: 0-9509289-5-X
978-0-9509289-5-1

Typesetting, layout and design: Oldtown Design
Proofreading: Antoinette Walker
Printing: GraphyCems

This publication was supported by the Arts Council.

Acknowledgements

First of all, we thank the authors of the various essays contained in this volume for their willingness to write the original articles for publication in *Children's Books in Ireland/Inis* and for their equally willing approach to updating their work for inclusion in this volume.

Mags Walsh and Jenny Murray from Children's Books Ireland gave much practical support to the project, and Seamus Cashman and the board of CBI and Sydney Blain, Principal of the Church of Ireland College of Education, and the board of CICE Publications, Mary Byrne, Geraldine O'Connor and Susan Parkes, are also thanked for their support.

The Arts Council is thanked for providing financial support for the publication.

Thanks are due too to Prof Kimberley Reynolds and Keith O'Sullivan for their words of encouragement when we were seeking funding for the project, and to Michael O'Brien of The O'Brien Press who gave useful advice.

A special thanks goes to PJ Lynch for the magnificent cover for *Irish Children's Writers and Illustrators*. His generosity and support are greatly appreciated.

— VC & SP

Contents

Introduction

Over the course of four years as joint editors of *Inis: The Children's Books Ireland Magazine* (initially *Children's Books in Ireland*), we commissioned a series of 'close-up' articles on the work of children's authors and illustrators working in Ireland at the time. These articles were published between autumn 2001 and December 2004, and this book is a collection of those *CBiI/Inis* articles.

We chose our subjects carefully at the time, with the aim of reflecting the best that Ireland had to offer and work that could stand scrutiny at an international level. Naturally, things have changed in some ways in the meantime: some authors represented here have ceased to write for children or now publish very little; on the other hand, some authors not included in the series have by now accumulated a significant body of work and no doubt would have been included had the series continued.

However, we took the decision to confine this publication to the articles actually published in the series, on the grounds that, whatever its short-comings, the series represents a snapshot of excellence in Irish children's literature in English at the turn of the 21st century, and although it is not the complete picture, we felt it was worth preserving the snapshot intact. We have asked the contributors to update their articles to cover recent work by the authors and illustrators concerned, but otherwise the book is exactly equivalent to the series, with the lacunae this inevitably entails.

All the writers/illustrators are Irish by birth, background or affiliation – as indeed are the contributors. Many of the books discussed in the articles, however, were not published in Ireland. The series began when the crest of the wave of Irish publishing for children had been reached, and the wave was beginning to curl back on itself. In the 1990s there were close to ten publishers of books for young people active in the Irish market, and there was certainly a boom of sorts in publishing for children. This may have been an astonishing phenomenon in its time, but it was hardly a 'golden age' (Cruickshank 2001).

From the vantage point of the present, it is easy to see that the so-called boom had more quantity than quality to it: though some very fine books were published at that time – and most of them are discussed here – there were also many that might have been better never to have left their authors' computers, and it is neither surprising nor lamentable that some of these authors are no longer writing.

The sudden growth in output can be explained largely as a response to a combination of commercial and social stimuli: rising literacy levels, increased affluence, a renewed pride in Irish identity (the World Cup and *Riverdance* phenomena belong to the same period), economic growth and, not least, a schools-led demand for Irish content in books for children that could enrich a curriculum that was opening up to the idea of imaginative literature's role alongside textbooks and factual accounts of history, for example. This is typical of developing national children's literatures the world over: children's literature grows out of and eventually away from books whose main role is in the classroom. So it is not to be wondered at that there was such an outpouring of historical novels for children at this period. Doubtless many of the authors were genuinely interested in addressing themselves to Ireland's past and to important historical events that had hitherto been off limits to children's authors, such as the Great Famine or the 1916 Rising, but it is also indisputable that publishers were eager to publish books for children that would find a ready market in Irish schools, and to have Irish-based authors available to speak in schools and libraries, which would be a sure boost to the marketing strategy. The roaring success that was Marita Conlon-McKenna's *Under the Hawthorn Tree* was not only emblematic of this new interest in Irish historical fiction for children but was probably the marketing model upon which the production of such large quantities of it was based – though, gratifyingly for its author, none of the books that came after it enjoyed anything like its commercial and popular success.

Perhaps inevitably, given the quantity of output at the time, much of it was at best classroom-oriented and at worst of a low standard, poorly edited and badly marketed (Coghlan and Keenan 1996). Some of the publishers concerned were enthusiastic but unprofessional in their approach to the business side of publishing, and could not survive; there were good reasons for the demise of others, in many cases related to the adult rather than the children's side of their publishing. Whatever the reasons, the loss of some of the publishers who were publishing for children ten or fifteen years ago has doubtless been a contributory factor in the relative silence of some of our best writers in recent years, while other publishers are hardly to be regretted.

Today, there is a single house publishing in English consistently for a youth market in Ireland, and a few that spurt out an occasional volume in a rather half-hearted manner and whose output is generally as uninspiring as it is irregular. If the boom of the 1990s was built on shaky foundations and doomed to collapse, the current situation is not ideal either. Irish children's writers and Irish child readers have to rely on a single indigenous English-language publishing house to meet their needs – on the one hand the authors' need to be published in their own country and the opportunity to write what we might term vernacular work for their young fellow citizens; and on the other, the children's need for a literature that is at least partly set in their own country and about characters and situations with which they can readily identify. There are some indications that new small publishers with an interest in children's books are starting up, but they have yet to prove themselves in the market.

This volume deals with those working mainly through the medium of English and the publishing phenomenon discussed is an English-language one. Conditions in the Irish-language publishing world are quite different, but it is inspiring to note that some of the most innovative publishing taking place in Ireland today is through the medium of Irish. For example, the only graphic novels for a young audience produced here are Colmán Ó Raghallaigh's splendid publications.

The current situation is that many books by Irish authors and almost all books by Irish illustrators are published outside Ireland. But how serious is this leakage of Irish talent to foreign shores? Certainly the publishers feel aggrieved that the authors they nurture through their early work are later snapped up by British and American publishing houses, after their worth has been established at the expense of their Irish publishers, as the publishers see it. This is true of the adult as well as the children's publishing world, and is probably an insoluble problem in an overwhelmingly Anglophone country sandwiched between two Anglophone world centres of publishing.

More disquieting is Celia Keenan's argument (2007 and also touched on here, in relation to Eoin Colfer's work) that the globalisation or international-isation of Irish writing for children may tend to rob the work of its Irish voice – though she does note here the beginnings of a return to his Irish roots in Colfer's most recent work. On the other hand, Matthew Sweeney, whose work has always been published in Britain, himself acknowledges that his voice has been shaped by the oral Irish storytelling tradition, so perhaps this tendency to deracination among Irish writers published outside Ireland is not quite as worrying as Keenan has suggested. What is quintessentially Irish may have more to do with quality of language and imagery rather than blunter manifestations such as the use of identifiable Hiberno-English, an Irish setting or references to a recognisable traditional Irish way of life. And, Emer O'Sullivan in a paper presented at the launch of Children's Books Ireland (CBI) in 1997, commented on 'the special situation and function of Irish children's literature since the early 1980s' remarking that '[i]n the process of establishing itself, this literature doesn't want to, nor does it have to, satisfy all the wishes and needs of young Irish readers'.

In any case, economic concerns are likely to ensure that Irish authors, for children or adults, will be tempted away from Irish publishers, as long as the Irish market remains small and Irish publishers find it difficult to make inroads into British and American markets. Sarah Webb (2003) and Marie-Louise Fitzpatrick (2003), both writing in *Inis*, have commented on the limitations of publishing in a small country, highlighting the general lack of professional support felt by authors and illustrators. They advocate more co-editions and partnership agreements with British publishers, rather than any drawing back from publishing in an international market. Translation rights to books by Irish authors are sold internationally, and it is not unusual to see names familiar to Irish readers on the shelves of bookshops in Tokyo and Toulouse, Beijing and Bratislava.

Perhaps there are other reasons why Irish literature for children has changed in recent years, reasons that have little to do with place of publication. Mary Shine Thompson (2003) argues that children's literature has traditionally been used to acculturate, educate, improve and transmit ethnic, national, class and gender values. In a changing Ireland some of what has been traditionally seen as desirable and worthy of transmission has become diffuse and complex. Many Irish children today grow up in homes where the latest electronic devices, expensive holidays and all sorts of material goods are the norm. A day spent harvesting turf on the bog is more exotic to most Irish children today than the idea of a trip to Lapland at Christmas to visit Santa. An Ireland that is populated by 'decklanders', as David McWilliams (2005) so cuttingly puts it, doesn't seem to have much call for books with a particularly Irish tone. Writers also have to be careful to observe issues around child safety; it is not so easy now to let young Eily or Jimín ramble unaccompanied along boreens and up and down mountains, or alone along city streets, even in the pages of fiction.

It would be mean-spirited indeed to wish upon children the litany of the 'miserable Irish childhood' so relentlessly depicted by Frank McCourt in *Angela's Ashes,* but the theme of unhappy youth proves popular in writing for adults, attested by the success of John McGahern's novels and memoir. Other adult authors are currently presenting an image of Ireland that reflects the confidence and improved social and material lives of inhabitants in the early 21st century; some of this is in the pages of 'chick lit', a genre at which Irish female authors have become remarkably successful, and which is possibly the antithesis of miserable youth, or at least of youth miserable due to economic or social hardship. There has been little popular corresponding 'girly' fiction for younger readers emanating from Irish sources, and overall there is little recent comment, implicit or explicit, on modern Ireland in Irish children's books (see for example Níc Ghabhann (2004), where it is argued that current Irish children's literature does not meet the challenges of a changing Ireland). This may be partly explained by the requirements of the classroom, which, whether people are prepared to admit it or not, still tends to dominate Irish children's publishing output. At the same time, many schools and libraries are now most concerned with stocking books and other resources that reflect the ethnic and cultural background of the 'new Irish', but few books set in Ireland feature children whose racial origins are not 'traditional' – and where they do, these characters tend to be cast as asylum seekers or refugees, rather than as characters whose skin tone or ethnographic characteristics just happen to be different from the majority. It takes time, of course, for social change to work its way into fiction, and doubtless we will see such characters in future books by Irish writers for children.

Another problem of a small market, or rather of a small national community and an even smaller literary one, is that reviewing tends to be too kind. As editors of *Inis* we found it difficult to get reviewers to be anything other than complimentary about Irish-produced books, or even about books published elsewhere by Irish authors and illustrators. While such an attitude might be thought admirably supportive, the lack of constructive criticism inevitably encourages the production of the mediocre and does nothing to educate authors, publishers and readers about how writing, illustrating and editorial and publishing standards might be improved or developed. As Aubrey Flegg (2001) has said, 'authors … need to be conditioned to accept a much higher level of benign criticism in reviews'. Publication outside Ireland has a role to play in toughening up Irish authors, who cannot expect kid-glove treatment from British or American reviewers. Reviewing of children's books in main-stream Irish media has improved in small ways, with occasional reviews of particular titles in the newspapers, but as a rule, children's books tend to be lumped together for mass treatment from time to time – a practice that forces reviewers to write brief notes about children's books rather than to give a considered review. There seems to be a tendency to think that the function of reviewing of children's books is promotion of titles rather than provision of thoughtful accounts that might be of use to discriminating adults in choosing books for their children.

If the move from writing and publishing books with an Irish 'accent' or a particularly Irish setting has been widely remarked, little attention has been paid to the lack of opportunity for Irish young people to read books translated from other languages. This is an unfortunate feature of all English-language-dominated markets, and it is perhaps ironic that children who grow up speaking less used languages are exposed to a wider range of books, because translation is considered normal in their cultures, and so they have easy access to books originally published in a variety of languages.

There are other lacunae too: there is a shortage of good picturebooks from Irish sources, and Irish poetry for children is also thin on the ground, though Mary Shine Thompson (2002) is hopeful that a new tradition of Irish poetry for children may arise. The three picturebook artists discussed here, Marie-Louise Fitzpatrick, Niamh Sharkey and PJ Lynch, are all published outside Ireland, though Fitzpatrick's early books were published here, and some of Lynch's books have been published in Irish co-editions. This is largely due to Irish publishers' caution about taking on the expensive process of picturebook production, and perhaps too to the traditional Irish valorisation of word above image, whereby novels and short stories sell better than picturebooks. *Something Beginning with P*, published by The O'Brien Press in 2004, magnificently bucked both the illustrated book and the poetry trends: this is a stunningly illustrated collection of Irish children's poetry published by an Irish publisher – a unique publishing event in this country.

Though Irish publishing for children has long passed its peak in volume terms, other areas of the children's books world are gaining ground. Children's Books Ireland (CBI) plays an important role in the promotion and development of all aspects of children's books on this island, in many respects paralleling events in Irish writing, publishing and bookselling

(Coghlan 2006, 2007). Ireland has an active national section of the International Board on Books for Young People (IBBY). The Reading Association of Ireland awards and the CBI/Bisto awards for children's books have been joined by the Dublin Airport Authority award for children's books, a category of the Irish Book awards, and IBBY Ireland nominates books and authors for international honours. Awards may tend to over-rate some books whose value is questionable, and certainly in the past the Bisto awards have not always singled out the books that in retrospect might stand out, but there is no doubt that awards are a valuable tool for bringing books to public attention, and as such are to be welcomed as part of the children's books scene.

Perhaps the real 'golden age' of children's literature is now occurring not in the publishing houses and bookshops of Ireland, but in the universities and other academic institutions. The number of people writing about Irish authors and illustrators in this volume shows that there has been a remarkable growth in the numbers engaged in the study of children's literature. Irish children's literature after about 1950 was disgracefully overlooked by the canonising *Field Day Anthology*, an indication that it still has a long way to go to find acceptance by the literary elite, but in the space of only a very few years, children's literature has not only found its place in university departments of English but in some cases is a mandatory part of English literature syllabi, while it continues to be a core part of teacher education. Postgraduate courses are on offer too, and children's literature is increasingly researched at doctoral and postdoctoral levels. The Irish Society for the Study of Children's Literature produces books of academic articles based on its annual conferences which touch on or focus on Irish writing for young people. Irish scholars regularly contribute papers on Irish children's literature to academic conferences in Ireland and at international conferences around the world, and in 2005 the International Research Society for Children's Literature held its biennial congress in Dublin, providing an opportunity for Irish people interested in the study of children's literature to be exposed to a wide range of high-quality papers and seminars.

Following Ireland's re-naissance as a wealthy nation, whose young people are among the most cosmopolitan in the world – though also with a worryingly increasing population of alienated young people who are racked by drugs, violence and physical and intellectual poverty – it will be interesting to see where Irish children's literature will go to in the next ten years.

— VC and SP, Dublin, February 2007

References

Cashman, Seamus (ed) (2004) *Something Beginning with P: New Poems from Irish Poets* O'Brien Press

Coghlan, Valerie and Celia Keenan (eds) (1996) *The Big Guide to Irish Children's Books* Dublin: Irish Children's Book Trust; see also Valerie Coghlan and Celia Keenan (eds) (2000) *The Big Guide 2: Irish Children's Books* Dublin: CBI

Coghlan, Valerie (2006/2007) 'A Brief History of CBI' pt. 1–3 *Inis* 18, 19, 20

Conlon-McKenna, Marita (1990) *Under the Hawthorn Tree* O'Brien Press

Cruickshank, Margrit (2001) 'Is the Golden Age Over?' *Children's Books in Ireland* 27

Fitzpatrick, Marie-Louise (2003) 'Pushmi-Pullyu; Author-Publisher' *Inis* 5

Flegg, Aubrey (2001) Letter in *Children's Books in Ireland* 27

Keenan, Celia (2007) 'Divisions in the World of Irish Publishing for Children: Re-colonization or Globalization?' in Mary Shine Thompson and Valerie Coghlan (eds) *Divided Worlds* Dublin: Four Courts Press

McWilliams, David (2005) *The Pope's Children: Ireland's New Elite* Dublin: Gill & Macmillan

Nic Gabhann, Áine (2004) 'Hardly Plotting Society' *Inis* 11

O'Sullivan, Emer (1997) 'Ireland and the World of Children's Books' *Children's Books in Ireland* 16 and 17

Thompson, Mary Shine (2002) 'Begging the Moving Finger: Irish Poetry for Children – Is There Any?' *Inis* 3

Thompson, Mary Shine (2003) 'Is Children's Literature *Really* Literature?' *Inis* 6

Webb, Sarah (2003) 'What's Happening to Irish Children's Publishing?' *Inis* 5

Eoin Colfer

By Celia Keenan

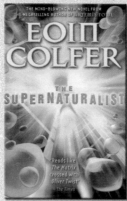

Titles by Eoin Colfer

Artemis Fowl series

Artemis Fowl: The Lost Colony (2006) Viking

Artemis Fowl: The Opal Deception (2005) Viking

Artemis Fowl: The Seventh Dwarf (2004)

(a short story for World Book Day) Viking

The Artemis Fowl Files (a companion book to the series) (2004) Viking

Artemis Fowl: The Eternity Code (2003) Viking

Artemis Fowl: The Arctic Incident (2002) Viking

Artemis Fowl (2001) Viking

Other titles

The Legend of the Worst Boy in the World (2007) Puffin

Half-Moon Investigations (2006) Viking

The Legend of Captain Crow's Teeth (2005) Puffin

The Legend of Spud Murphy (2004) Puffin

The Supernaturalist (2004) Viking

Ed's Bed (2001) O'Brien Press

The Wish List (2000) O'Brien Press

Ed's Funny Feet (2000) O'Brien Press

Going Potty (1999) O'Brien Press

Benny and Babe (1999) O'Brien Press

Benny and Omar (1998) O'Brien Press

Short stories

'Satellite Batteries' and 'The Two Mary Learys' (2001)

in Robert Dunbar (ed) *Skimming* O'Brien Press

Eoin Colfer

By Celia Keenan

The books of Eoin Colfer remind me of the line from Milton, 'Thousands at His bidding speed and post o'er land and ocean without rest'. Perhaps not quite thousands speed at Eoin Colfer's bidding, but all the figures that people his fiction from *Benny and Omar* through *The Wish List* to *Artemis Fowl: The Lost Colony* do. Indeed, there is something quite Miltonic too about the range of landscapes, from the heat and dust of *Benny and Omar* via a literal hell and heaven in *The Wish List*, to the icy wastes of *The Arctic Incident*, not to mention the subterranean hell-like magma-flare-dominated, unstable regions inhabited by 'The People', which, though they are offered as an alternative to the corruption of the earth, are really a fallen and fiery subterranean mirror image of the above-ground world of humans, or 'mud-men' as they are called. In this vertiginous restless world, the vision is not that of heaven and hell but of varieties of hell. Even Colfer's series of stories about Ed Cooper for younger readers reveal a world in which everyday objects like beds and toilets or feet and shoes are disconcertingly unstable.

When Colfer's first novel *Benny and Omar* was published, it received almost universal critical welcome. It was above all an extraordinarily fresh voice, that rare thing in contemporary Irish writing for children, a large comic voice. It was strikingly child- or, more precisely, boy-centred. It genuinely conspired with children over the heads of adults. A particular example would be the use of television-speak in *Benny and Omar*, which works extraordinarily well, and which children can be almost guaranteed to understand before adults do. Colfer's subsequent invention of gnomish script in the Artemis books, as well as his sophisticated use of high-tech, sci-fi, computer-generated and cinematic frameworks would be later developments in that same conspiracy.

Benny and Omar dealt with important themes such as loneliness, friendship and loyalty, difference and similarity. Unlike so many books that deal with foreign people speaking English, it acknowledged the very real differences in speech patterns. Above all, it dealt with the difficulties posed for boys in the contemporary world. It did all this in a genuinely funny way. It took risks in the current climate of political correctness. It had a genuine sense of rootedness. It spoke of Wexford, its cultural and physical landscape, its dialect and unusual word usages, and its passion for hurling. That local emphasis was essential to its universal theme, in that the reader could only understand Benny's deracination in Tunisia in light of the meaning of home for him. Colfer's book had all the important qualities that readers have traditionally expected from the best books in terms of theme, character, voice and setting.

The horror of Benny's move to Tunisia, and of compound life there were powerfully conveyed as was the enormous charm of the figure of Omar, who is encountered first in a classic all-boy, mock-aggression initiation ritual involving a broken hurley stick. The language of popular television programmes, through which the boys communicate, is finely sustained. The centre of the story, when Omar conveys his tragic family history in the words 'Homer, Marge: Thomas the Tank Engine – Boom' never fails to elicit either laughter or shocked silence.

The dusty landscape and the plight of children who live off the rubbish of the world is not evaded. Omar could be a victim, a rent boy, a beggar, but instead he is empowered with some of the magic of a figure from the *Arabian Nights* stories. He is independent, resourceful and highly civilised. He represents a truer masculinity than Benny's self-conscious machismo. In chapter nine, wearing formal dress, including his late father's colourful fez, he cooks a beautiful meal, says grace, and enacts the ritual of a festive dinner evoking his Islamic inheritance. Colfer deliberately pays homage to Mark Twain's *The Adventures of Huckleberry Finn* here, where, after the meal, the night falls, the boys watch the stars and Omar is plunged into a profound grief at the loss of his family in words that echo Jim's lament for his family in

Huckleberry Finn. Paradoxically, the impoverished and orphaned Omar gives Benny a glimpse of a fuller and bigger world than his own.

Colfer, like Twain, runs into problems with the enormity of the potentially tragic ending. He flounders in the floodwaters, seems to promise a sequel, but the sequel, *Benny and Babe*, although it too climaxes in flood waters, retreats from this story of difference and loyalty. An exotic pixie of a tomboy, Babe, replaces the romantic boy, Omar, in *Benny and Babe*, and rural seaside Wexford replaces the dusty desert of Tunisia as the locus of most of the action. Babe replicates the kind of challenges posed by Omar, purely physical challenges, especially in the ritual hurling game in the beginning. She is the classic tomboy, accompanied by a vicious mutt of a dog. She inflicts physical pain. She seems to be as deracinated as Omar. Though we are told she has relatives, we never see them or visit her home. Babe and Benny form an uneasy alliance, making money from collecting lost fishing tackle and challenging the local bully who tries to undermine their trade.

In the end, Benny's ambition forces him to take an excessive risk. He and Babe are almost drowned, and Babe is transformed from an honorary boy into a typical girl, who punishes Benny for his foolhardiness in stereotypical female fashion through her long silence and her refusal to visit him in hospital. That illustrates the danger of this boy–girl alliance. The transformation of Babe into an object of desire leaves the reader a little uneasy at the end. It raises very interesting questions about the construction of gender in Colfer's books. With the exception of Meg Finn of *The Wish List*, there is throughout his work a witty repetition of traditional male stereotyping of women. This includes the caricature of Jessica Shaw as the literature-loving amateur dramatic dilettante, oppressor of all masculine enterprise in both *Benny and Babe* and *Benny and Omar*, along with the brilliantly funny portrait of the trendy American teacher Harmony Rossi, who, in order to make Benny and his brother feel at home in their new school, says, 'Now you kids, how do we show these two Irish boys that we love them? – Group hug,' in response to which Benny's horror is shared by the reader.

Though Colfer stereotypes almost all his female figures from Jessica

Shaw through to Holly Short, Opal Koboi and Angeline Fowl, a subtle self-mockery functions as an ironic comment on it. This can be illustrated from *Benny and Omar*, where we are told that 'Benny wouldn't even admit to having a feminine side, never mind touch it'. Benny longs for the rough, masculine comfort of the hurley-loving, hide-tanning Christian Brothers in the face of this threat of being literally smothered by the feminine. Colfer performs a tightrope act over contemporary political correctness, and the spectator watches with open mouth, hoping he will keep his balance. He almost always does. Benny's brother George represents that effeminate 'other' that all 'real boys' fear, and Benny is a real boy.

Even in *Artemis Fowl* this play with gender continues. Who but Colfer would be so daring as to use the word 'fairy' both as a term of contempt and in its literal sense in a contemporary book aimed at the early adolescent? Who else would create an oversexed heterosexual sprite called Chix Verbil, who 'believed himself God's green-skinned gift to females' but whose delicacy of language and gesture suggests the feminine. Who would create the possibility of romance between a one-metre-high, catlike female leprechaun aged fifty and a fourteen-year-old human boy? Who else would depict such bizarre incestuous relationships as those between Artemis and his mother and between Butler and his sister Juliette? (For a detailed examination of the first three Artemis Fowl books see Keenan 2004.)

A developing tendency in the two Artemis books has been the increased use of scatological humour, which seems to function as some kind of pre-pubescent equivalent to a preoccupation with sex. It is given concrete form in the outlandish comic figure of Mulch Diggum, a thieving, earth-eating dwarf whose most powerful weapon is his anus. When Mulch lowers his bum-flap, no one is safe from his noxious emissions, as he farts and excretes his way through the earth and the narrative. This writing is a little reminiscent of Raymond Briggs or Roald Dahl at their most scatological, but exceeds them in concentration and lack of restraint. It is very much part of a laddish world and, as in the great comic tradition, Mulch's interventions are ultimately beneficial, comic rather than satirical, closer to Chaucer than to Swift. It is possible that the young reader will greet the arrival of Mulch with squeals of laughter and the adult reader with exasperation.

Eoin Colfer likes to live dangerously, artistically speaking. *The Wish List* is so subversive of traditional Judaeo-Christian iconography that it is surprising there was no adverse reaction from the fundamentalist or literal Christian lobbies. Angels, devils and saints are treated in the comic way that is only acceptable in the uniformly Christian world of medieval drama, where everyone shared the same belief, or in the contemporary post-Christian world, where there is no shared belief. The following are examples of how Saint Peter and Satan are depicted: '"You're cutting it pretty fine, Fabrizzi," commented Peter in flawless Italian. "The gift of tongues, another little bonus from the boss." Satan was crouched in a corner of his office, playing a gameboy. "Die, alien scum," he was saying feverishly, wiggling horny thumbs.'

Colfer's theology in *The Wish List* does not bear too close a scrutiny, though he could not be accused of fashionable anticlericalism. Indeed, his short story, 'The Two Mary Learys' contains a warm and kindly portrait of a Catholic priest, which seems particularly striking in the contemporary Irish context.

The deconstruction of folk and fairy lore in the Artemis books is much less radically subversive than that of western religion in *The Wish List*, as there is a long tradition of ironic postmodern versions of fairy stories, from Dahl through to Carol Anne Duffy. Indeed, Colfer alludes to one of the more contemporary Irish deconstructions of the leprechaun story when he lists Siobhán Parkinson's *The Leprechaun Who Wished He Wasn't* as one of his own favourite books. It undoubtedly influenced him in his Artemis books. It is a feature of his generosity of spirit that he acknowledges his sources and influences openly and in a way that is not always evident in other Irish children's writers.

The critical reception of *Benny and Omar* contrasted very strongly with that of *Artemis Fowl*, about which opinion is deeply divided, both in Ireland and abroad. In Ireland, the contrast between June Edwards's (2001) enthusiastic review in the *Sunday Tribune* and Brenna Clarke's (2001) review in *Children's*

25

Books in Ireland epitomised the divisions. Edwards found that 'Fans of high-tech gadgetry will love this novel which manages so artlessly to blend futuristic IT with fairy magic … The LEPrecons are characters whose complexities and insecurities are portrayed very realistically.' Brenna Clarke, in contrast, wrote, 'Colfer never creates the credible world of fantasy that is needed for magic to be believed'. Eileen Battersby in *The Irish Times* voiced similar reservations: 'Even on a second reading – I have yet to see its appeal and remain distanced by its knowing tone, the slickness, gimmickry, lack of magic.'

In Colfer's own list of favourite books, the first-named is *Huckleberry Finn*. In a rare comment on writing technique ('Eoin Colfer's Favourite Children's Books' 2002) he says he especially likes Twain's book for its quirky first-person narrative and says that he would like to try to write a first-person narrative himself. It is a very interesting comment. Colfer's own confidence with regard to voice, speech and tone suggest that he could handle a first-person narrative better than most writers who use the form today. However, the first-person narrative makes another demand than control of voice. It requires a genuine insight into the interior life, the thoughts and feelings of characters. Nothing that Colfer has published since *Benny and Omar* suggests that the interior life of characters is of particular interest to him. In fact, he has tended to move further away from engagement with it. There were instances of a felt life in *Benny and Omar* and, to a lesser extent, in *Benny and Babe*. *The Wish List*, with its comic moralising in the tradition of the morality play, its movement into a fantasy world (albeit based on religious iconography) and its frantic action, prefigured the overground/underground world of the Artemis books. *The Wish List* is the first book where he parts company with traditional realism in the narrative structure. *Benny and Omar* had magical elements, but its structure was conventionally realistic, and *Benny and Babe* was firmly in the realist camp.

Artemis Fowl marks a very dramatic change in Colfer's work and fortunes. In Colfer's case, the movement to a British publisher from an Irish one has brought tangible gains. Global success with its concomitant wealth, cult status, multiple websites and so on is not negligible. Nor is the more intense focus on plot and the higher degree of editorial and production polish. However, the losses are very great indeed. All sense of the national and local has been eradicated, or transformed into parody. Speech rhythms are entirely mid-Atlantic. No Hiberno-English or Wexford usages are evident. Landscape has become virtual. Wexford and its passion for hurling have vanished from the new map. Almost all culture-specific references have been eliminated. Though Colfer's material success is greater than that of other Irish writers for children, this tendency to globalisation seems common to almost all those who move from an Irish to a British publisher.

All truly great books, whether for adults or for children, speak out of their own cultures and thence to the wider world. Colfer lists books that he admires or loves, among them the works of Mark Twain, Harper Lee, Tolkien and Philip Pullman. Twain and Lee are quintessentially American voices, they 'sing America'. Tolkien and Pullman are correspondingly quintessentially English voices. That alone would not account for their greatness, but it is an important ingredient in that indefinable thing. The attempt to globalise literature for children leads to a very poor, dilute thing.

Colfer is imbued with ambition. His talents as a writer, which include energy, fearlessness, generosity, variety, comic inventiveness, linguistic facility and a love of popular culture, including cinema and technology, would indicate that he has the potential to create that thing that has remained elusive, the Irish children's classic that might be mentioned beside its counterparts of other nations. To do that he might need to return to 'The foul rag and bone shop of the heart' as encapsulated in *Benny and Omar*. There have been recent indications that he may indeed be doing just that. His 2004 novel, *The Supernaturalist*, combines a tight thriller plot, and an emphasis on gadgetry, with a sense of pain, grief and loss. The plight of orphan children is depicted with imagination and sympathy. Even though it is a decidedly modern, even postmodern, text it certainly reminded me in many ways of Dickens at his most compassionate, especially in *Oliver Twist*. The more recent Artemis Fowl books (*Eternity Code*,

Lost Colony) are considerably less violent than the earlier books. In fact in a recent interview (Rix 2006) there is a clear indication that this change is a deeply conscious one on Colfer's part; the realisation that his children would one day read his books also made him rethink violence: there is a graphic fight in the first book, but 'I decided there was no need for that really ... Now there are chases but not much actual violence'. The amorality of his hero, the criminal boy genius, worried the new father in him too. Over the next four books Artemis developed a conscience. Colfer, in the same interview, goes on to speculate that that very conscience may spell the end for Artemis, in artistic terms: 'I don't know how much longer he has in him ... once he gets completely good, that's it.' Artemis in fact faces two threats to his existence, becoming good, and growing up. There are many humorous references to incipient puberty throughout the books, but most explicitly in *The Lost Colony*. Artemis flirts with puberty and then retreats to the comfort of pre-adolescent maleness.

It is certainly interesting that Colfer titled his most recent Artemis book *The Lost Colony*. That colony is a mythic Irish one. Perhaps Ireland may be found again in the Artemis universe, or perhaps Colfer is inviting postcolonial theorists to join in the fun!

References

Battersby, Eileen (2002) Review in *The Irish Times* 25 May

Clarke, Brenna (2001) Review in *Children's Books in Ireland* Summer

Dunbar, Robert (2002) 'Interview with Eoin Colfer' *Books for Keeps* 137

Edwards, June (2001) Review in *Sunday Tribune* 19 October

'Eoin Colfer's Favourite Books' Guardian Unlimited © Guardian Newspapers Limited (2002) www.books.guardian.co.uk (accessed June 2003)

Eoin Colfer's Official Website http://www.eoincolfer.com/home.htm (accessed February 2004)

Keenan, Celia (2004) 'Who's Afraid of the Bad Little Fowl' *Children's Literature in Education* 35 (3)

Rix, Juliet (2006) Interview with Eoin Colfer *The Guardian* 14 October

Marie-Louise Fitzpatrick

By Lucinda Jacob

Selected picturebooks by Marie-Louise Fitzpatrick

Silly School (2007) Frances Lincoln

I Am I (2006) Roaring Brook

Silly Mummy, Silly Daddy (2006) Frances Lincoln

You, Me and the Big Blue Sea (2002) Gullane

I'm a Tiger Too! (2001) Wolfhound/Gullane

Izzy and Skunk (2000) David & Charles

The Long March (1998) Wolfhound

Peadar Ó Laoghaire (1996) *Séanna* Cois Life

The Sleeping Giant (1991) Brandon (republished by Wolfhound/Merlin)

An Chanáil (1988) An Gúm

Marie-Louise Fitzpatrick

By Lucinda Jacob

One of our most successful and long-established writer-illustrators, Marie-Louise Fitzpatrick has been creating award-winning picturebooks for almost twenty years now. She lives and works in Dublin where she trained in visual communication at the College of Marketing and Design (now part of the Dublin Institute of Technology), and indeed her first book, *An Chanáil*, was set in Dublin. While entirely her own, I find Fitzpatrick's illustrations are reminiscent of two of my other picturebook heroes: Helen Oxenbury and Jan Ormerod.

There was such excitement when *An Chanáil* came out. Winner of the Reading Association of Ireland Book award, and Bisto Book of the Decade 1980–1990 (Irish language category), it was published by An Gúm in 1988 and I still remember well the thrill of picking it up in the bookshop and realising as I opened it that here was a ground-breaking title. It was the first time, that I could remember, that a recognisable local landscape was used in an Irish picturebook, and with a narrative that was clearly contemporary. No matter that I would have to get out a dictionary to read it! I was living in Rathmines at the time, only yards from the Grand Canal, and so picking out well-known and much-loved landmarks from the illustrations proved irresistible as I turned the pages. Places such as 'The Dungeon', one of the terraced houses, bedecked in bric-à-brac and in itself a work of 'outsider art', were obvious and are particular to the place, but more importantly from the point of view of the book which would have a readership beyond the canal communities, these features that can be recognised only by those who know this stretch of the canal are used by Fitzpatrick to give a sense of place which is both setting and starting point for the story.

It has been said that the canal itself is the central character in the story, and perhaps the sheer 'liveliness' of the broad scene makes it seem so. The extended horizontal of the landscape format, with the double-page spread open as the pages are turned, means the focus is on the illustration rather than the words, and so the canal is writ large. However, I would contend that one of Marie-Louise Fitzpatrick's strengths is that her narrative is strong: she does know how to tell a story; in this case the story of a dog lost and found, and the trip that its young owner takes in a canal barge to thank the people who found him way out on a rural stretch of the canal.

Fitzpatrick's second title, *The Sleeping Giant*, is also rooted in a real place, and the sleeping giant is actually an island off the Dingle peninsula known locally as 'the dead man' – exciting again for our little family as we recognised it from our holidays. Anecdote aside, it was also something completely new to Irish readers; a large format, full-colour picturebook. Looking back on the book now it is clear that Marie-Louise was cutting her teeth on these early titles, and for instance she is more trusting of her pencil line in these illustrations than she was in *An Chanáil*, and she no longer feels the need to outline the figures in ink. The story is stronger too. My then four-year-old took it entirely in her stride, and really hers was the target age. It is a child who solves the giant's problem, and in this Fitzpatrick shows an evident and early understanding of the importance of the centrality of the child in children's books. Interestingly, it proved really quite scary for my two-year-old, as the giant rose up out of the sea and created havoc in the modern landscape full of holidaymakers. Unable to articulate it at the time, the same daughter, now seventeen, remembers it well and thinks it was the poignancy of the giant's situation (he's too big to fit into our world and has to be persuaded back out of it) that made it all the more affecting, making him more real and thus more scary and yet to be pitied (a subtle and complex combination of response) despite his benign rather cuddly appearance.

Between, or rather while working on, her picturebooks Fitzpatrick has worked on a number of other projects, producing numerous covers for

books by other authors, such as Maeve Friel's *The Deerstone* and many titles for Wolfhound Press, notably illustrating Aislinn O'Loughlin's humorous series of inverted fairy tales in jaunty black and white line drawing, and several titles for Poolbeg Press, including *Anna's Six Wishes* by Margrit Cruickshank. In all of these, her ink drawings serve to entertain and ease the eye of the reasonably confident new reader. Other bread-and-butter projects included illustrations for a reading scheme featuring 'Emma' and 'Joe', and here she was an inspired choice. Champions of 'real' books in teaching children to read often cite the fact that in picturebooks, as opposed to 'readers', the pictures support the reader as they carry meaning, often as much or more meaning than the words themselves do, and Fitzpatrick was certainly alive to her experience as picturebook maker in her approach to these titles. So often young children find that a reduced text can be difficult enough to decode and the judicious use of well-matched illustration makes the task of learning to read simpler and more satisfying as they 'read' the pictures alongside the text. In 1991 she illustrated the poetry anthology, *Rusty Nails & Astronauts,* edited by Robert Dunbar and Gabriel Fitzmaurice and published by Wolfhound. Some of the illustrations are colour, but most are black and white wash, giving shades of grey. Colour or not they are all sensitive; she avoids an interpretive approach, rather they enhance by suggestion and mood. Fitzpatrick continues to illustrate occasionally for other authors – for example, *Dear Tooth Fairy*, written by Pamela Duncan Edwards (Katherine Tegen Books), and *Jasmine's Lion* by Angela McAllister (Doubleday).

Bringing together her skills as researcher, storyteller and illustrator, her picturebook, *The Long March*, was again an arresting piece of work. And with its appearance it became clear to those that follow these things that this was a writer-illustrator who is not afraid to pursue a train of thought that, though fascinating to her, might not at first seem a likely subject for a picturebook. And she is not afraid to set herself some stiff challenges in the process. The story is based on a snippet from the margins of the history books, namely the astonishing fact that in 1847 when the Native American

Choctaw people heard of the potato famine here in Ireland they responded by raising 170 dollars, a sizeable sum. They were by no means wealthy themselves and their motivation seems to have stemmed from a feeling of empathy for their fellow humans, no matter that they were European and therefore in some sense the enemy. In fact it is the central character's ambivalence in the face of the news from Ireland that makes the story dramatic and holds our attention as we wonder whether the young man will side with those who speak warlike words or those who urge compassion. That he does the latter and acts out of altruism is what makes the story important for the reader. The Choctaw heard that Irish people were dying as they walked the roads in search of food and it clearly resonated with their own experience. Fitzpatrick initially researched the story from Ireland, but she realised that she needed to go to the Choctaw and speak to them herself. This proved most fruitful as she was able to take copious numbers of photographs for reference and she was able to use real people as models for her characters and inspiration for the way she would tell the story. Her choice of pencil rather than colour for the illustration was refreshing and entirely appropriate for such serious subject matter, and it also allowed her to demonstrate her skill in its use. The illustrations are sensitive and in places she makes great use of the white space on the page. One of my favourite spreads is the one showing the Choctaw struggling uphill across the page in a strong diagonal, the desolation of their situation emphasised by the expanse of white. In some portraits the drawing is somewhat static, but this appears here to be a matter of stylistic choice rather than flaw and I can only admire the magnificent drawing of the Grandmother, a modern-day elder dressed, as they all are, in traditional clothing. Fitzpatrick received a number of well-deserved awards for *The Long March*: the Reading Association of Ireland Special Merit award, the Bisto Book of the Year award and mention on the IBBY Honours List, and with it she entered the American market for the first time.

In 1996 she illustrated *Séanna*, a storybook by Peadar Ó Laoghaire, first published in 1910 and brought to life for a new generation of Irish-

Izzy was afraid of making mistakes...

but Skunk wasn't.

"I'm a boy," said the boy.   "I'm a boy like you."

language readers with her fluid watercolours depicting character and action dispersed through the text.

Izzy and Skunk, her next picturebook, was published in America as well as in Britain and Ireland (for some reason best known to themselves UK and US publishers renamed it *Lizzy and Skunk)* and it won the Bisto Book of the Year 2001, and in the US it was a School Library Journal Best Book of the Year. In it she returns to the landscape format and to a younger audience. Izzy is scared of things like shadows in the dark, but her toy skunk isn't, and through this narrative that is founded on acute observation of how toys are used by young children as vehicles for emotions that they find difficult to articulate, Izzy deals with her fears as she explores the world about her in a busy robust manner. This empowering text is enlivened by illustrations that show a new fluidity of line and sureness of touch in their use of watercolour, which is evident in all Fitzpatrick's subsequent work to date.

I'm a Tiger Too! was shortlisted for the Bisto Book of the Year in 2002, and again it is a picturebook for younger children. Again Marie-Louise shows her instinct for what is important to children of this age and the story is a deceptively simple one where the makebelieve becomes real as the lonely little boy at the centre imagines playing with a cat-become-tiger, a dog-become-wolf and so on until he meets another little boy with whom he can really play 'tigers'. The overall design is a delight, and together with Fitzpatrick's fluid line and sure use of watercolour, mentioned earlier, it is one of those productions where everything seems to be in place and all the elements are pulling together to tell the story in such a way as to be almost invisible to the reader. It just seems right.

With *You, Me and the Big Blue Sea*, Marie-Louise's storytelling skills are again to the fore. I do not mean by this that the writing takes precedent – far from it, much of the meaning is conveyed by the illustration and it sets up a tension between text and picture which makes the book absolutely scintillating. I am aware that this description may seem overblown but I believe this is the essence of what is meant when people talk of the

'excitement' of reading, whether you are reading words or pictures or, as in this case, both. The writing is nicely arch, with an adult narrator giving a voiceover to the illustrations which show rather more to the reader than the narrator is herself aware of, thus showing that she, the adult, has missed the point. This is of course utterly delicious for the child reader and a classic element in books for children. It was the joint winner of the Bisto Book of the Year 2002/2003 and is published in Britain by Gullane and in the USA by Roaring Brook.

In some of her most recent books for young children published by Frances Lincoln, Fitzpatrick has created an engaging character, Beth, who in the first two titles has to be roused out of her bad mood in *Silly Mummy, Silly Daddy* and out of her negative feelings about school activities in *Silly School*.

Her recent book, *I Am I*, is a painterly picturebook with a sophisticated yet simple concept at its centre. Two little boys find that words spoken in aggression lead to violence and destruction, and so, remorseful, they find a way to state their identity, 'I am I', in a way that respects the other's boundaries. This concept is worked out visually with a simplicity that belies the research and thought that went into its creation. Fitzpatrick states that the initial idea came from a saying and related symbol of the Native American Choctaw, and which she reproduces in a note at the back of the book. Interestingly, this note gives us an insight into the working practice of the artist as she explores an idea and material from one work (*The Long March*) in another quite different creation. This story is parable-like, using few words and the style of illustration is also a new development in Fitzpatrick's work. The medium is acrylic paint and it gives a richness and depth of saturated colour to the landscape and the two boys. The aggression of the words is emphasised by a wonderfully inventive use of orthography; the words feel almost scratched in black, spiky and broken line, and these black lines actually take to the air and become birds, then more menacingly, barbed wire and eventually a destructive dragon-like monster. Thankfully, the word *sorry* is also powerful and rejuvenating, and

as it falls to the ground seedlings which become red poppies appear. The parable is brought to a close through a couple of changes in scale, first showing the boys on a glowing planet, and then as if from an aerial photograph, in their adjoining front yards, thus asking the reader to think where the story might take place.

Marie-Louise Fitzpatrick has rarely produced a book that has *not* won awards, and it is a credit to her dedication to her craft and her career that she is at last achieving the international recognition that she deserves.

Maeve Friel

By Celia Keenan

Titles by Maeve Friel

Witch-in-Training: Flying Lessons (2002) Collins
(and sequels, 'for confident young readers')
Felix on the Move (2000) Franklin Watts
The Lantern Moon (1996) Poolbeg
Distant Voices (1994) Poolbeg
Charlie's Story (1993) Poolbeg
The Deerstone (1992) Poolbeg

Short stories

'The Bonfire War' (2001) in Robert Dunbar (ed) *Skimming* O'Brien Press
'The Chanctonbury Ring' in *Shiver* (1994) Poolbeg

Adult non-fiction title

Here Lies: A Guide to Irish Graves (1997) Poolbeg

Maeve Friel

By Celia Keenan

Maeve Friel's is one of the quieter voices in Irish children's literature. Perhaps for that reason her work has not quite received the attention it deserves. Yet two of her four novels were shortlisted for an RAI award, three have reached the shortlist in the Bisto Book of the Year competition, one was awarded a Bisto Merit award and her books almost invariably receive favourable reviews and remain in print.

Her work is a little difficult to categorise. *Charlie's Story* is utterly contemporary in its setting and its concerns. The others are to a greater or lesser degree engaged with the past. *The Lantern Moon* is a pure historical novel, whereas *The Deerstone* and *Distant Voices* are more concerned with the ways in which past and present interact with each other. Her two short stories ('The Chanctonbury Ring' and 'The Bonfire War') also reflect this concern.

One feature which seems common to all her work is a distinctive and powerful sense of place. In *The Deerstone* the combination of water and stone (the latter whether natural or manmade or even miraculous) is what anchors the story in a Glendalough that is vivid and recognisable. Contemporary urban Dún Laoghaire in a state of development which makes it resemble a building site forms the appropriate rough background to *Charlie's Story*. *Distant Voices* is set in the physical space of the border between Northern Ireland and the Republic of Ireland, between Derry and Donegal. Much of *The Lantern Moon* is set in Ludlow and along Offa's Dyke, which forms the ancient and deliberately defensive border between Saxon and Celt, between England and Wales. 'The Chanctonbury Ring' uses an Iron Age fort in the south of England to create a ghostly tale in which the past literally comes to life. 'The Bonfire War' is a very allegorical, almost impersonal morality tale in which village rivalry about the matter of who can create the biggest bonfire is enacted between the children of North Hill and South Hill. The conscious use of the popular phrase highlighted by Seamus Heaney 'whatever you say, say nothing' signals very clearly to the reader that the contemporary Northern Irish dispute forms the real background to this story. Even *Felix on the Move* (2000), Friel's story for younger children, locates place at the centre of the action. It dramatises the importance of the most significant place in children's (or cats') lives – home. It confronts that great trauma of moving house. It asks and comfortingly answers the question, what really constitutes home?

Place in Friel rarely exists as mere background. In the story about Felix the cat, it *is* the theme, and in different ways the same thing is true of each of her novels, though the answers to questions are not necessarily comforting. In *Distant Voices* what is being interrogated is the spirit of the place itself. Its shifting landscape of earth and water and vulnerable manmade structures seems to contain within it the shifting story of courage and sacrifice, loyalty and treachery that is constantly re-enacted from the earliest times to the present day.

Here Lies: A Guide to Irish Graves (1997) was written for adults but it could be very useful in doing local history with children. This book explores some of the stories reflected in Irish monuments to the dead. It is not to suggest that there is anything morbid about Friel's work to say that the grave is something that has a powerful presence in almost all her books. In *Charlie's Story* the London underground, sleeping place of young Charlie along with crowds of other homeless people, is described as a necropolis: 'It was like another city down there, crowded with bodies almost touching one another, but each in its own carefully guarded space.' The smell and feel of the grave recur from the Glendalough of *The Deerstone* to the rough Viking grave of *Distant Voices* where Ellie McLoughlin digs with her hands to touch the body of a thousand-year-old murdered boy. In 'The Chanctonbury Ring', the ringfort of the title is the burial place of generations of the dead. In *The Lantern Moon* William and Annie Spears stand beside the graves of their dead mother and little sister at the turning point of the story, and later on they find shelter when they are entombed in the crypt of a ruined abbey near Hay on Wye.

Broadly, Irish writers for children can be divided into two groups: those who see the duty of the writer as being to protect children and to transmit heritage to them (writers like Eilís Dillon, Michael Mullen and Tom McCaughren fall into this group) and writers who seek to liberate children from the burden of the past and embrace modernity (Margrit Cruickshank, June Considine and Tony Kiely would represent this tendency). Maeve Friel does not fit comfortably into either group. Her attitude to the past is complex and ambiguous. In *The Deerstone* this complexity can be clearly seen. The hero, Paud, is angered by the neglect of his parents. In this time-slip novel he finds consolation in the past by finding a kind of doppelgänger in the form of Luke, son of Dermot McMurrough in the years before the Norman invasion of Ireland. The Glendalough of that time is a frightening place, threatened by civil war between the O'Tooles and McMurroughs. Looting and burning are commonplace. Hope is very firmly placed in the hands of modernisers in that war-torn world. If they do not succeed chaos will ensue. 'Those like Dermot and Laurence who stand for change and progress will be driven out and instead the old exhausted ways will prevail, dragging our province back into the darkest ages.' Incidentally, it is difficult to avoid the allusion that these words make to contemporary difficulties in Northern Ireland. But Friel's seeming rejection of the past is balanced by the fact that she endorses its value, both by revisiting it frequently as she does in her historical novels, and by the use of overt statements such as that in *Charlie's Story* where Charlie thinks: 'If you don't know your own history you don't know who you are.'

It is possible to trace a growing confidence and sureness of style in Friel's work. Her first novel, *The Deerstone* (1992), though interesting in its theme and setting, had some of the awkward features that many time-slip novels display, such as the difficulty of conveying a modern child into the past, the dependence on artefacts such as watches and snacks to signal modern time and the difficulty of balancing past and present. Her depiction of the twelve-year-old hero's character lacked something in depth, though his situation was conveyed convincingly. What worked well were the linking of myth and history – the story or legend of the deerstone itself, the use of the deerstone, the use of the twin-motif and the image of the nurturing deer. In other words the poetic elements succeeded best and were most memorable in this novel.

In *Charlie's Story,* Friel used a first-person narrative to tell the story of a fourteen-year-old girl's search for her own story and for survival. There is a gritty realism here and very little room for poetry. Charlie is surrounded with affectionate, bumbling, inadequate adults: her father, her two uncles and her grandmother. She had been abandoned in early childhood by her mother. She is viciously bullied at school. The difficulty of finding a resolution to Charlie's dilemma is great, and the plot causes problems. The emphasis on physical rather than psychological bullying is too great and the resolution is somewhat unsatisfactory. However, the thing that is truly memorable in this novel is the portrayal of the interior life of the heroine. Charlie's self-loathing is very convincingly depicted. Unlike the clichéd descriptions of teenagers looking in mirrors and moaning about spots or freckles common to much teen fiction, the descriptions of Charlie's self-mutilation as she persistently tears at her hair or eats her fingers almost to the bone are painful to read.

Friel does not flinch from the terrible. Charlie is barely saved from suicide by outside intervention. Though the actual bullying depicted may be some-what extreme in its physical manifestations, and the bullies may be rather stereotypical, the current consoling notion that if a child confides in an adult all will be well is resolutely and realistically rejected. Friel admits the hard fact that most children know and most adults don't want to believe: telling an adult can often exacerbate the problem for the bullied child.

Though very different in setting and theme, *Distant Voices* builds on the achievement of the two earlier novels. It side-steps all the pitfalls of the time-slip form by having a ghost from the past coming to haunt the modern world. In the time-slip novel one of the greatest evasions is death itself. The time-slip works by pretending that the dead are not dead, the past is not gone. In *Distant Voices* the dead and death are ever present, and yet the living adolescent girl can help the dead Viking boy by safeguarding his remains and by telling his story. The plot is very tightly controlled. The isolation of the heroine is conveyed: 'At least she was no longer alone. Her parents were back from work.' Her interior life, her dreams and desires are carefully evoked. The time of year, between Hallowe'en and the winter solstice, makes a perfect background for a ghost story. Wind and flood threaten the world. The political border becomes at once a psychological border and the border between life and death. A deliberate reference to the actual Hallowe'en massacre at Greysteele near Derry makes the link between ancient and modern worlds explicit. There is nothing that is mere surface here. The institutional forces in the form of gardaí and archaeologists sound a somewhat banal note at the end, but Ellie's comment that the Viking boy 'need have no fear of being forgotten again' is what is important.

The Lantern Moon visits another past, this time the beginning of the 19th century in Ludlow in the north of England. It is more classically a historical novel than *The Deerstone* or *Distant Voices*. Its greatest achievement is the vividness and truthfulness with which the lives of poor working people are depicted. The intense physical pain of child labour is exquisitely conveyed in the description of the work of five-year-old Libby Spears: 'Her fingers ached as she pushed her little needle through the fine cream kid leather, taking care not to puncture it or, worst of all, stain it with blood, for she often pricked herself.' The world described is a random and chaotic one in which parents are lost, children are sentenced for minor theft, passions are aroused in an instant and the terror of mob rule is always present. This latter feature, the irrationality of the mob, is shared with *Charlie's Story* and *Distant Voices*. William and Annie Spears, after the tragic burning to death of their mother and little sister and the destruction of their home in Ludlow, set out on a harrowing journey to find sanctuary finally in Australia. The young people are not individualised to the same extent as those in *Charlie's Story* or in *Distant Voices,* and that seems perfectly appropriate in this historical novel set in a time when modern individualism was not rampant, and when the poor could not afford to be in any sense individual. It is as if the children represent all poor and oppressed children. The plot is tightly controlled. The language is spare. The weather, particularly the terrible winter cold, is palpable. The ending of the novel in which the children's father is restored to them almost miraculously by fire, the force that took their mother and sister away, is perfectly in tune with the theme of the novel. If the world is chaotic, wonders can happen just as easily as tragedies.

In fact fire, with its destructive and its redemptive connotations, is an almost constant motif in Friel's novels. It represents destruction itself in *The Deerstone,* where the roofs of Glendalough burn twice in an orgy of tribal hatred. In *Distant Voices* the burning ritual of a Viking cremation is at once beautiful, loving and murderous. The images of the burning effigy of Napoleon Bonaparte, the burning home of the Spears family, and the raging bushfire of the final pages accumulate poetic meaning, which become symbolic in *The Lantern Moon,* and finally in Friel's short story 'The Bonfire War', the image represents the folly of human rivalries wherein people would often get more satisfaction from their rival's defeat than from their own victory.

Although Friel's voice is quiet, it is also thoughtful and significant. She has developed her craft carefully. She has written about the most important things. The Troubles of Northern Ireland are subtly reflected in almost all her work. She is a truthful writer who in her novels and short stories has offered few easy solutions to the public and private dilemmas of the late 20th and early 21st centuries.

PJ Lynch

By Valerie Coghlan

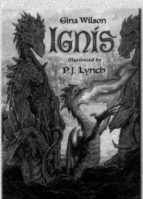

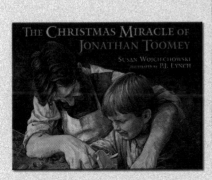

Selected picturebooks by PJ Lynch

Charles Dickens (2006) *A Christmas Carol* Walker
Frank R Stockton (2003) *The Bee-man of Orn* Walker
Marie Heaney (2002) *The Names Upon the Harp* Faber and Faber
Gina Wilson (2001) *Ignis* Walker
Douglas Wood (1999) *Grandad's Prayers of the Earth* Walker
Amy Hest (1997) *When Jessie Came Across the Sea* Walker
Mervyn Peake (1996) *Boy in Darkness* Hodder
Brendan Behan (1996) *The King of Ireland's Son* Walker
Susan Wojciehowski (1995) *The Christmas Miracle of Jonathan Toomey* Walker
Antonia Barber (1994) *Catkin* Walker
Hans Christian Andersen (1993) *The Snow Queen* Andersen Press
East o' the Sun and West o' the Moon (1991) Walker
Hans Christian Andersen (1991) *The Steadfast Tin Soldier* Andersen Press
Neil Philip (ed) (1990) *WB Yeats Fairy Tales of Ireland* Collins
E Nesbit (1989) *Melisande* Walker
Alan Garner (1988) *A Bag of Moonshine* Collins

PJ Lynch

By Valerie Coghlan

When he won the Kate Greenaway Medal (presented by the UK Library Association) for the second time in 1997, PJ Lynch joined an elite group of picturebook artists. To win that medal once is an outstanding distinction, and the list of winners since the medal was first presented to Edward Ardizzone in 1956 is a roll call of the very best artists whose work has been published in the United Kingdom. But to win twice brings Lynch into the company of Raymond Briggs (his former teacher at Brighton College of Art), John Burningham, Charles Keeping, Janet Ahlberg, who are all giant figures in picturebook illustration. The books which won the Greenaway Medal for Lynch were *The Christmas Miracle of Jonathan Toomey* and *When Jessie Came Across the Sea*. *The Christmas Miracle* was also the winner of the Children's Books Ireland/Bisto Book of the Year (1996/7) award and the Reading Association of Ireland's 1997 award. It is likely that he hasn't appeared on the winners' lists more often only because of the inadequacy of Irish book awards in evaluating picturebooks.

Lynch has an international reputation, especially in the United States, and has won and been shortlisted there and elsewhere for many awards. It was his first award, the 1987 Mother Goose (now discontinued) – presented to the most exciting newcomer to British children's book illustration – that set him on his career as a picturebook artist. Presented for his pen-and-ink illustrations accompanying Alan Garner's text for *A Bag of Moonshine*, this prize marked Lynch out as an illustrator to be noted. It is, however, as a watercolour artist and illustrator that he is now chiefly recognised. His skill in achieving depth and luminosity in this medium is remarkable. His paintings are highly textured: wrinkles on hands and faces and fur on animals are finely indicated, and garments flow and ripple around their

wearers. The fall of light too is a characteristic of much of Lynch's work; it is frequently denoted with touches of gouache, sometimes investing his subjects with an almost ethereal being. Equally, absence of light and the casting of shadows is used to give heft and significance to scenes in his books; Lynch's worlds and characters are frequently emphasised and atmosphere is created through contrasting dark with light, bright with sombre.

Lynch still works occasionally in black and white. His sketches and silhouettes for WB Yeats's *Fairy Tales of Ireland*, published in 1990, added to his reputation, and in 1996 he illustrated *Boy in Darkness* by Mervyn Peake, a brave step given that Peake himself was a talented artist with a bent for the macabre.

But Lynch's own fluid lines and sensitive shading can impart a sense of menace and threat and sometimes hilarity. The great Arthur Rackham was one of Lynch's earliest influences and the lessons learned from Rackham are noticeable in Lynch's work. Both artists are adept at conveying foreboding, and both have a liking for juxtaposing conventionally beautiful characters with ugly, often grotesque figures as a means of highlighting fantastical or magical elements of a narrative. Lynch too, like a number of other illustrators, including Anthony Browne and Angela Barrett, gives an occasional nod to Rackham as he blends distorted human faces into the trunks of trees, for example, increasing the sense of foreboding when the daughter finds herself in a gloomy wood in *East o' the Sun and West o' the Moon*, or underscoring the tussles between the giant and Art in *The King of Ireland's Son*. Edmund Dulac, Maxfield Parrish and Norman Rockwell are other artists whose influence Lynch acknowledges, and nods to the American artists' work can be found in some of Lynch's books of the late 1990s in particular.

Lynch is not a subversive picturebook artist; his illustrations do not run counter to the tale told by the text. Nor, in most of his books, do his pictures bear the weight of the narrative. His work complements the verbal telling, and expands the story by showing the world inhabited by the characters and by giving them substance and expression, and in so doing brings an extra depth and richness to a story. We see the Languid Youth

(who bears more than a slight resemblance to Oscar Wilde) becoming less languid in *The Bee-man of Orn*; or we are in Jonathan Toomey's little wooden house as the widowed woodcarver weighs the risk he is taking by allowing laughter and love into his life once more; and close looking reveals Lou, Jessie's husband-to-be, observing Jessie in shipboard scenes before they actually meet.

Many of the stories illustrated by Lynch are traditional, some set in fantastic worlds, and others in a world of fairy tale or myth. He has worked with texts by a number of 'classic' authors whose work has been illustrated by other artists, and Lynch shows that he is capable of bringing a new dimension and visual interpretation to these. Hans Christian Andersen's *The Steadfast Tin Soldier* is a good match for Lynch's style, and the picture of the soldier falling to the pavement from on high will stick in every reader's mind. His illustrations for Oscar Wilde's tales match Wilde's elegance: they are formal, gorgeous and distant with none of the interplay with character shown in his illustrations for Yeats's tales.

Realistic narratives illustrated by Lynch are also often set in the past, as in *The Christmas Miracle of Jonathan Toomey* and *When Jessie Came Across the Sea*. *Grandad's Prayers of the Earth* is closer to modern days, but the world depicted here is a timeless rural world for whose preservation the book is a plea. It is essentially a romanticised, even sentimental American landscape. Other books show the influences of European romantic painting, especially in backdrops like the mountains, caverns and craters of *Ignis,* where again the 'normal' beauty of the world known to humans and the secret, fantasy world of imagined creatures (in this case dragons) are paired with each other; witness the eye contact in the scene where Cara, the young girl, and the dragon, Ignis, say goodbye as each steps back into their own worlds.

The gaze is a characteristic device of Lynch's, used to express feelings and highlight tensions between protagonists. Throughout *Christmas Miracle*, characters look with significance at each other – for example when Thomas argues with Toomey about the sheep he is carving – and there are varying emphases in the gaze between Toomey and the widow McDowell.

Jessie too speaks with her eyes, whether she is showing her skill as a lacemaker or reading a letter from her grandmother. Here, in a classic picturebook device, we are situated with a character who gazes out of a window as we are directed through Jessie to look at the street scene below, and to reflect on the phrase in her letter that 'there are too many people in America and the streets are not gold'.

While he is adept at portraying beauty, one of PJ Lynch's strengths as a picturebook artist is his ability to convey the bizarre: ugly, distorted and deformed characters also inhabit the worlds created by Lynch. In *East o' the Sun and West o' the Moon,* the Long-nose and all the company of Trolls show Lynch's work at its most grotesque. Their near-relatives appear in the battle scenes in 'Moytura', one of the tales in *The Names Upon the Harp*, a book of Irish myths and legends, and their forebears were surely present at the christening of the baby princess in Melisande. Here the fairies gather expressing their pique at not being invited to a party to celebrate the birth of the princess. These fairies are robust and malevolent, owing something to Rackham and Rossetti. Melisande, published in 1989, was one of Lynch's earliest picturebooks. In it we have foretastes of characters and themes that are developed in later books, like the sailing ships pitching in stormy waters, which are displayed with much more assertion in *East o' the Sun.*

Storm-tossed sailing ships feature too in *When Jessie Came Across the Sea.* A small panel on the left of the opening shows Jessie's grandmother standing on the quay edge, looking towards a larger panel which shows the ship bearing Jessie to America. Text on both pages divides the panels, the gap heightening the sense of loss experienced by the grandmother and signifying the possible turbulence ahead for Jessie in her new life. As well as viewing them from afar, the onlooker is brought onboard to follow the voyage bringing young Jessie from her Eastern European home across the Atlantic to New York and a new life. The artwork in this book is a *tour de force.* Every page opening displays different aspects of Lynch's artistic capabilities: the landscape and cityscapes, the crowds as the travellers anxiously watch for sight of their promised land, and most of all the sensitive portrayals of

Jessie as she grows from a timid immigrant to a confident young woman. How she develops as she begins to earn money, enough to pay for her beloved grandmother to join her in New York, and as she attracts the love of a young man are displayed in a splendidly nuanced series of pictures showing Jessie and the new land and life to which she must adapt if she is to survive.

A painterly style such as Lynch's is favoured in the United States and his work is acclaimed there. Survival, of the person and of the land, is emblematic of the American dream. This theme underlies *The Christmas Miracle of Jonathan Toomey, When Jessie Came Across the Sea* and *Grandad's Prayers of the Earth*. Jonathan Toomey finds family and, it is implied, religious faith; Jessie finds prosperity and love; and the boy in *Grandad's Prayers* finds peace through the natural world. In these books the hint of menace, of something lurking in the undergrowth or at the back of a cavern, that we observe in some of Lynch's other work is absent. Instead, he draws together the strands of questioning, search, catharsis and ultimately resolution, creating artwork that is celebratory and affirming.

The ability to capture emotion is shown to great effect in *Christmas Miracle*. This also allows Lynch great play in showing interiors – warmly lit by the fire and oil lamps – and it must rank with *Jessie* among Lynch's finest accomplishments. The story is warm-hearted, but it barely skirts the sentimental. This highlights what must always be a difficulty for PJ Lynch: he is, to some extent at least, confined by the text with which he is working. Avoiding sentimentality is a close call for a painter working in a traditional style, and this is one of the remarkable things about *Jessie*. Hest's text is flat and distanced; Lynch catches the warmth implicit in the story of a young emigrant Jewish girl, and measures his narrative intent in illustrations that have the potential to become overblown but never do.

Similarly, in *A Christmas Carol* Lynch conveys with equal dexterity Scrooge's terror at his visitations by the ghosts and the Cratchits' desperation and eventual rejoicing. Here we again see the crowded street scenes at which Lynch excels, although he finds them wearying to paint, and we can

contrast them with the deserted landscape of winter and graveyards. The match of Charles Dickens and PJ Lynch seems like one made in heaven and it is likely that the PJ Lynch-illustrated edition of this quintessential winter tale will rank as one of the classics. One has to wonder, if, having been paired once with him there will be other alliances with Dickens; *Great Expectations* would seem to have been written for PJ Lynch to illustrate.

Portraying love or tenderness while avoiding sentimentality creates visual tension in telling a story, and Lynch references the work of Pre-Raphaelite artists as a touchstone to present love, romantic and physical, in particular in some of his earlier books. Sexual attraction is nuanced in scenes in *East o' the Sun and West o' the Moon*, when at first the Prince observes the Princess sleeping; then, when the Princess sees that the man in her bed is 'the loveliest Prince one ever set eyes on'; and ultimately, with a nod to Klimt's 'The Kiss', when the Prince recognises that the Princess is the woman to be his bride: 'So there was great joy and love between them all that night.'

Lynch again shows the influence of the Pre-Raphaelites in *Catkin*, the story of a little cat who undertakes a journey to the Land of the Little People to free a changeling child, but this time the journey is one into a fairy-tale land of great beauty. Arts-and-crafts-style motifs decorate the pages, highlighting the Celtic otherworldliness of the land of the dark Lord and his Lady. Some of the characters are physically recognisable from other Lynch books, presumably because in the early stages of drafting his work Lynch uses models and photographs. These rather stylised and sometimes stilted human figures are particularly evident in his earlier illustrations for fairy tales and fantasy. Characters in his later work generally show more fluidity and individuality; they are recognisable human beings, not just stereotypes in a story. Lynch's style shows development in moving away from the framed scenes that were more apparent in earlier work, into double spreads, which are often bled to the edges. He often uses the page as a means of conveying the time and space through which characters travel and in which the action takes place; this technique gives Lynch's work a narrative integrity of its own, independent of the text, and the reader is subsumed into the story.

PJ Lynch's *The Bee-man of Orn*, has many recognisable Lynch motifs. Here we see the familiar earth colours glowing warmly on the pages, and the use of green, bright and vivid on the trousers of the Languid Youth or murky and mysterious when the sorcerers are gathered together. The wide open landscape scenes are reminiscent of *When Jessie Came Across the Sea*, and the towers and spires far off across the plain are reminders of the castle (rather like the Rock of Cashel in County Tipperary) on the opening page of *The King of Ireland's Son*. The Bee-man himself is an undoubted relative of the little old men in that same book, and there are plenty of Lynch's trademark angled scenes, allowing readers to view the action from beneath and above. It is a long book at 48 pages. There are many full-page illustrations and double-page spreads and almost every page carries at least a smaller illustration. The text of this lengthy story is accommodated in many instances in boxes and panels, and in others it is integrated with the illustrations. This attention to the design of the whole page, making each page-turn a surprise and a delight, is also typical of much of Lynch's work. Stockton's story of an old man who sets out to discover what it is from which he has been transformed, only to find he was once a baby, demands much of an illustrator, and Lynch is in good company here. The story was illustrated by Maurice Sendak in 1964. For any artist to follow in the footsteps of Sendak would be a challenge, and it is one to which Lynch has risen. Stylistically quite different, these two artists have in common a ferocious integrity in relation to their work, and a desire to reach the essence of the story they are illuminating.

Setting is important in Lynch's books. These are often theatrical in their presentation and interpretation of events, perhaps in part due to the intensive research into period dress, furnishings and setting that he conducts in preparation for starting work on a new book. Lynch takes detailed photographs of models on whom he then bases his subjects. Computers assist him in some of the more mundane aspects of his picture-making, but the fine detailing in his work always means that it is slow to produce, and PJ Lynch books do not appear with great frequency.

In many of his books he moves from one spectacular backdrop to another, imposing upon them characters who may be grotesque, humorous or romanticised. In some cases – *The King of Ireland's Son*, for example – there is an element of burlesque. The action moves quickly and, compared to other Lynch books, the romantic element is underplayed. Scenes between Art, the eponymous son, and the giant are full of movement, whether it is Art scaling the tree while the giant watches from on high or Art kicking the giant into the air and compelling the reader to turn the page to see where he lands, or in the final scene at the wedding party.

Lynch also does occasional work painting theatre posters and he has designed postage stamps for An Post. The year 2006 marked a departure from watercolour or ink, when he painted in oil two enormous panels depicting scenes from Gulliver's adventures in Lilliput. These were commissioned by Cavan Public Library and in one of them Gulliver towers over buildings familiar to residents of Cavan. It would suggest that a retelling of Gulliver illustrated by Lynch might be another heavenly match.

Lynch is a major picturebook artist, but like many artists who do not write their own texts, he is, to some extent at least, bound and possibly limited by the stories he selects to illustrate. Overcautiousness or even a stasis in what he does must always be a concern for an artist like Lynch. The children's book world now thinks it knows what it might expect from PJ Lynch and this may be inhibiting for him. Lynch is an artist in the classic mould, one who is capable of tackling great themes, but he also shows a flair for the comic and the ridiculous. It would be interesting to see more of this in his work. His ability as a draughtsman lends itself in particular to the freer, more quirky style of illustration that is seen in his pen-and-ink drawings and at times in *The Bee-man of Orn* and *The King of Ireland's Son*. With pen or brush he can mine emotions, create drama, provoke laughter; he enables his audience to see visions and to dream dreams – and sometimes nightmares. The worlds of PJ Lynch are varied and splendid and we may not yet have seen all of them.

Sam McBratney

By Liz Morris

Selected titles by Sam McBratney

You're All My Favourites (2004) Walker

In the Light of the Moon and Other Bedtime Stories (2001) Kingfisher

Once There Was a Hoodie, with Paul Hess (1999) Macdonald (Wayland)

One Grand, Sweet Song (1999) Mammoth

Just You and Me (1998) Walker

The Dark at the Top of the Stairs (1996) Walker

Guess How Much I Love You (1994) Walker and O'Brien Press

The Chieftain's Daughter (1993) O'Brien Press

You Just Don't Listen (1994) Mammoth

(originally published as *Put a Saddle on the Pig* 1992)

Funny, How the Magic Starts (1989) Mammoth

Short stories
'Blind Chance' in Robert Dunbar (ed) *First Times* (1997) Poolbeg

Poetry
Long, Tall, Short and Hairy Poems (1996) Hodder

Sam McBratney

By Liz Morris

Probably best known for his award-winning and best-selling book, *Guess How Much I Love You,* Sam McBratney is one of Ireland's finest and most prolific writers, with radio plays for adults, and over seventy-five children's titles published by a range of the most respected Irish and UK publishers. His books are nationally and internationally acclaimed and his awards include the American Booksellers' Association's prestigious ABBY award, the UK Reading Association award and Ireland's Bisto Merit award. Like his fellow Ulsterman, Martin Waddell, he has written picturebooks for the very young, highly popular novels and short stories for newly independent readers, along with some challenging and thought-provoking books for older readers. His poetry collection *Long, Tall, Short and Hairy Poems* remains popular with teachers and pupils around the country while 'Blind Chance', his contribution to *First Times,* a collection of short stories for young people by fifteen Irish authors, is one of the finest and most thought-provoking in what is an outstanding anthology. Nothing less than a lengthy dissertation could do justice to the many works of such a versatile and productive author, so this short article will examine only a few of his best-loved books.

If any theme can be said to link McBratney's work in the titles below, it is that of family life. While it is far from unusual, of course, for authors to present the characters in picturebooks as safe and protected in loving family units, McBratney does evoke strongly the warmth and security experienced by the young when in the care of loving and supportive elders. *Guess How Much I Love You* – which, since its publication in 1994, has sold over fifteen million copies worldwide and has been translated into forty-five languages – has a reassuring message that the reciprocated love of parent and child is measurable in universal terms. Personally, I feel this book has been rather over-rated, especially in comparison with other titles by this author, but the rhythmic text, as Little Nutbrown Hare tries (and fails) to outdo his father in protestations of love certainly makes this ideal for reading aloud. Anita Jeram's simple and warm illustrations contribute in no small way to its enduring appeal and popularity with adults and children alike. Ten years later, the two again worked together to produce *You're All My Favourites*, a tender bedtime tale that was shortlisted for the Bisto awards, in which mother and father bear confront the anxieties and insecurities of their offspring, reminding each of their special and unique qualities, and reassuring them that parental love is unconditional.

Other McBratney picturebooks, too, deal with the love and protectiveness of grown-up, often male figures for their young – in *Just You and Me,* Big Gander Goose respects Little Goosey's desire to shelter from the storm far away from other woodland creatures, rejecting repeated offers of refuge so that they can be alone, just the two of them. *The Dark at the Top of the Stairs,* also illustrated by Ivan Bates, features a wise old mouse that teaches his young charges a valuable lesson by allowing them to explore and discover, under his watchful eye, the dangers that lurk outside the security of the family home. In *In the Light of the Moon and Other Bedtime Stories,* an extremely attractive collection, illustrated with great humour and understanding by Katie MacDonald Denton, and written especially for bedtime shared reading, the eight stories provide children with the opportunity to explore with the grown-up reader emotions such as jealousy, fear and dependence in a reassuring, comforting and above all very safe manner. In each of these books, the tone is respectful of children and favourably disposed towards a family life in which the figures in authority give the young the space to learn for themselves: to be selfish, as with Little Goosey, or curious and foolhardy, as with the three small mice.

My own feeling is that McBratney's novels for older readers represent his best work, and here too the parents play a far more significant role in their children's lives than do many parents in novels for teenagers. In *Funny,*

How the Magic Starts, the narrator, fifteen-year-old Monica, addresses her parents as Mummy and Daddy and seems, at times, almost a product of a bygone age in her compliance with and respect for her parents' wishes. Although initially reluctant to meet the new boy next door, she agrees to do so when Mother and Father join forces over the mushroom soup at teatime. And her parents are proved right as the friendship with eccentric and witty Seymour Brolly develops from an inauspicious start to the point where Monica discusses with her mother the 'Great Compulsion that comes over people to find themselves a partner'. Her relationship with a family which, though frequently exasperating, is secure and loving allows Monica to ignore the jibes of those friends who sneer at the unconventional Seymour. Even when she does eventually rebel against her parents, rushing out and screaming that they don't understand her, her brother quickly appears to bring her home. And while she realises that the family will not 'be the same again: not exactly' she does apologise for the scene. Humdrum and stable family life, observed with a great deal of humour and insight, is the backdrop against which the adolescent Monica develops her relationship with Seymour.

In what, in my opinion, is McBratney's finest work, *The Chieftain's Daughter,* which won a Bisto Merit award on publication, family life again plays an important part, although in this case the growing love of the young protagonists develops in the tribal rather than the nuclear family. Once again the advice of the elders of the community is heeded and respected in this story of a love doomed by suspicion and hatred. Set in a vividly depicted Ireland during the very early years of Christian teaching in that land, narrator Dinn Keene tells the visiting 'Patrick of the Pens' of the gradual awakening of his love for Frann, daughter of Ard Bruill the chieftain. The secret meetings of pagan priest Corag Mor with the daughter of neighbouring chieftain Ogue have heightened existing tension between the two tribes: the feud 'had boiled the blood so that nothing would cool it'. Bruill's pleas that the 'children are not part of [the dispute]' are ignored, as are the new teachings voiced by Ancell, and the consequences are tragic for all concerned. Dinn Keene, now an old man, is left with only the memories of that 'great moment' when he became 'important in another person's eyes' and, just as Monica, some fifteen centuries later, describes that moment of recognition as 'like the element in a kettle when the power goes on. Like magic, really', Dinn remembers that 'even the Lake-dwellers appeared … in a different colour … yes, indeed, she showed me the colour of the wind.' Reprinted by The O'Brien Press, unfortunately with a cover that does the book little or no service, this is one of those books to which the term 'classic' justifiably applies.

The bitter results of conflict between neighbours which underlies *The Chieftain's Daughter* is present too in *You Just Don't Listen,* an anthology of short stories which also won a Bisto award under its original title *Put a Saddle on the Pig.* Sixteen-year-old Laura's father was a victim of 'mistaken identity', killed in 'a booby-trap explosion' many years before. Her mother routinely turns on the local radio news 'in case someone she knew had been killed'. In a very real sense, she and her mother are victims of the failure of generations of communities to heed words like those spoken by Ancell when he begged Ard Bruill to give his tribe the choice to live 'as people respecting one another in a great family as God-all-Father commands…' When Laura's mother, Victoria, decides to leave the city in order to be closer to Jim Mulholland, a man who has had 'strong feelings' for her for many years, Laura deliberately invokes memories of her dead father by speaking of the importance of 'a pair of young laburnums', saying that they are symbolic of 'former times … Other days … when Daddy was alive.' She continues this psychological battle against the proposed move by painting a picture of those 'lemon-coloured fronds' planted by her father, and places on her dressing table an old photograph of him landing a pike on the 'lough shore near Ballynahinch'. In a subtle reference to the ongoing political troubles of the city, her teddy bear is given a placard to hold, 'a triangular flag with three words written on it: Teddy Says No'.

Victoria understands the 'grand allusions', recognises that Laura is indicating, none too subtly, the 'wilful destruction of [her] emotional landscape' and resists Jim's pleas that she confront the issue directly. Jim, she feels, is 'too used to straight talking … to see that there is almost always more than one way of doing things…' She herself believes that 'some situations can be complicated in unimagined ways' and knows that both mother and daughter have choices to make.

At first Laura insists that she will stay in the city, that she will not be moved out of her own place to a farm near Bangor: until she is forced to consider leaving it, Laura has 'never been struck before by the significance of the place' and McBratney powerfully conveys this deep attachment to the streets, the houses, the gardens that are part of her 'mental landscape, her patch, home'. Her mother argues forcefully that in a few years' time she'll 'go away and stay away like everybody else' but it is not until Laura visits the Mulholland farm that she sees her mother's 'lost, familiar world' and realises that to 'tap into the well of hate she felt within … would be a wrong thing to do, unambiguously wrong … It would be to choose darkness'.

Unaware of this revelation, her mother chooses to sacrifice the chance of personal happiness, writing to Jim that she cannot be with him, that she cannot be sure Laura would put down roots again, that she's 'just not brave enough to make another start'. Having read this letter, Laura understands fully the depths of her mother's love for her. She vindicates the decision made by Victoria 'after Bob died … to make her daughter into an independent person; an individual'. The secure bonds of family love have given Laura the strength to argue, to disagree, to rebel and ultimately to make a difficult but wise decision.

A close-knit family again features in 'Sheffield' – a short story first published in 1979 in *Lagan Valley Details* and reprinted in McBratney's wonderful collection *One Grand Sweet Song* – although this family is much constrained by neighbourhood political and social beliefs. At seventeen, Hazel can 'hardly remember when the Troubles started'; she has lived all her life with the presence of the British army whose local base she can see from her bedroom window. When she meets a soldier, not much older than herself, she likes him, thinks he's different and 'quite exciting to think about'.

He cannot tell her his name, 'for girls led [the soldiers] into traps sometimes' but she calls him Sheffield, after his home town, a place where it would be possible for them to go for a walk or a drive in the car, where they could meet without fear of reprisal. But feelings in the area are running especially high with the death of a former neighbour, knocked down by an army patrol, and Hazel's own brother is involved in the riots that follow. Unable to meet her friend openly or regularly, Hazel tries to put her feelings for Sheffield into a letter she writes him: 'I pretend we're in a circle with strong invisible walls and I'd like to keep them there so that they can't get at us.' But in order to be together, they must both leave the place described by her mother as 'an awful place to live', a 'place that will drive [us] mad' and, though distressed by her parents' deep-rooted objections, Hazel chooses to join her soldier on his leave in Sheffield.

McBratney is a very fine and truly versatile author – and recognised as such by literary critics – whose work is enjoyed by readers young and old. He writes of ordinary people who live in ordinary circumstances, sharing as families and neighbours the difficulties that at times upset and disrupt their lives. His books reassure readers that the young and vulnerable in society can be encouraged by loving family to face whatever threats or insecurities the world may present. A consummate storyteller, he writes in the foreword to *In the Light of the Moon and Other Bedtime Stories* that 'reading to children, reading with them at the quiet end of the day, just feels to me like one of the most natural and worthwhile things you can do'. The benefits of reading to children, he suggests, may last 'for all of a lifetime'. But older children too need reassurance, need to discover for themselves that, as Laura's mother makes clear, 'there's more than one truth'. McBratney's books, sympathetic, warm and complex, provide that reassurance by exploring many of the truths of human experience.

Elizabeth O'Hara

By Ciara Ní Bhroin

Titles by Elizabeth O'Hara

Hurlamaboc

(2006, under the name Éilís Ní Dhuibhne) Cois Life

The Sparkling Rain (2003) Poolbeg

Penny-farthing Sally (1996)Poolbeg

Blaeberry Sunday (1994) Polbeg

The Hiring Fair (1993) Poolbeg

Hugo and the Sunshine Girl

(1991, under the name Éilís Ní Dhuibhne) Poolbeg

The Uncommon Cormorant

(1990, under the name Éilís Ní Dhuibhne) Poolbeg

Elizabeth O'Hara

By Ciara Ní Bhroin

Like many other distinguished writers of children's literature, Éilís Ní Dhuibhne, who later adopted the pseudonym Elizabeth O'Hara for her children's books, began her career as a children's writer by writing a story for specific children, her own two sons, then aged five and seven. Already an established writer for adults, Ní Dhuibhne distinguished between writing for adults and for children, highlighting the difficulty in the latter case of achieving that delicate balance between being oneself and understanding what it is to be a child (Ní Dhuibhne 1990).

Her first children's book, *The Uncommon Cormorant*, a humorous, episodic story relating the fantastical adventures of a young protagonist called Ragnar, was written 'with a sense of liberation and fun, not to mention truancy and subversion' (Ní Dhuibhne 1990). Since the best children's books are indeed liberating and subversive (particularly of adult assumptions about childhood), *The Uncommon Cormorant* was written in the right spirit, though one senses that the desire to tailor the story to the particular tastes and experience of specific children may have taken precedence over questions of structure and form. Ragnar's fun-loving grandmother is the first of a number of Nordic characters to feature in O'Hara's novels, all of whom bring a fresh and usually liberating perspective to bear on the lives of her protagonists. She is also the precursor to many strong, intuitive female figures, who often possess special semi-magical powers.

A desire to make available to Irish children a story that was a significant part of their tradition in the past was the motivation behind *Hugo and the Sunshine Girl*, a retelling of the folktale 'Maighdean an tSolais' ('The Maiden of Light'), which Ní Dhuibhne heard in the Donegal Gaeltacht and first recorded and transcribed in 1978. Her introductory note to the reader, explaining both the origins of the story and the style of retelling, has resonances of Lady Gregory's dedication to the people of Kiltartan in *Cuchulainn of Muirthemne* (1902) and places Ní Dhuibhne in the tradition of translation begun by writers of the Revival. *Hugo and the Sunshine Girl* features a heroine who comes to the hero's rescue and anticipates the emphasis on female heroism and the rich use of folklore and legend that are strong characteristics of O'Hara's subsequent fiction.

It was with her finely crafted, award-winning historical trilogy, consisting of *The Hiring Fair, Blaeberry Sunday* and *Penny-farthing Sally* – for which she adopted her pseudonym – that Elizabeth O'Hara came into her own as a children's writer, writing as much, one senses, for herself as for a juvenile audience. Her choice of genre is a popular one among Irish writers for children, whose desire to reinterpret Ireland's past for young readers is hardly surprising. Recent debates regarding nationalist and revisionist historiography indicate not only the central importance of history to postcolonial national identity, but also the way in which ideology inevitably colours any construction of the past. The past is necessarily constructed or invented in the present. Published in the 1990s, at the approach of the new millennium, against a backdrop of peace initiatives in Northern Ireland and growing national economic and cultural confidence, the trilogy returns to a culturally significant and inspirational era a century earlier, when the nation was yet to be imagined.

Spanning the last decade of the 19th century, the trilogy relates the maturation of a Donegal girl, Sally Gallagher, 'Scatterbrain Sally', from hapless schoolgirl to responsible young working woman, employed initially as a hired girl in Tyrone at the height of the Parnell/Kitty O'Shea scandal and finally as a governess in Dublin in the early days of the Revival. While the emphasis is on private rather than public history, personal and social destinies are subtly interwoven throughout. The vulnerability of child-workers and of females in particular is emphasised by O'Hara's stark depiction of the dehumanising hiring fair, which Sally likens to the slavery depicted in *Uncle Tom's Cabin*. The difficulties for Catholic girls working for

Protestant employers at a time of political and sectarian division is conveyed, often obliquely, through the ambiguous portrayals of Robert Campbell and Willie Stewart. The hardship suffered by Sally's sister, Katy, as a migrant worker in Scotland is one of a number of incidents highlighting the sad fate of many working women, whose stories went largely unrecorded.

While O'Hara evokes with great subtlety the joys and sorrows of growing up and the plight of the vulnerable in an unjust society, the overall tone is one of hope and possibility. Sally is resilient, resourceful and imaginative, a girl on the threshold of womanhood at a time of national awakening. The role of narrative in this dual awakening is cleverly explored. As with many engaging heroines of children's literature, Sally's love of story is central to her development. While her upwardly mobile friend, Maura McLoughlin, may have social opportunities denied to Sally, it is clear that she will nevertheless always be stunted by the limits of her own imagination. Sally embodies the heroic Revivalist values of self-invention and moral autonomy in the face of the provincial materialism of the emergent middle class, which the McLoughlins represent. By comparison, both of her suitors are less than heroic. Manus, incapable of generating his own moral frame of reference, is unable 'to make a great sacrifice on her behalf' while Thomas's patronising proposal is reminiscent of Darcy's to Elizabeth Bennet. Indeed the comment of the midwife, Annie Borland, regarding men – 'as soon as there's a spot of trouble they're away' – is indicative of the weakness of many of the male characters who populate O'Hara's books and who seem unable to muster heroism at times of crisis.

Joe Cleary's (2002) observation, in *Literature, Partition and the Nation State*, that 'the state divide conditions the imaginative horizons of Irish writers on both sides of the border', would seem not to apply to O'Hara, whose characters move freely between north and south. Indeed Sally's journey from the Donegal Gaeltacht to Tyrone and finally to Dublin is the reverse of Ragnar's trip with his grandmother in *The Uncommon Cormorant*, which encompasses a fantastical flight along Dublin's coastline, a rather sinister meeting with British soldiers (whom Ragnar significantly mistakes for Germans) in 'Oh Ma', County Tyrone, and a camping expedition in the heart of the Donegal Gaeltacht, where Ragnar puts his Irish to good use. A particularly intriguing image in *The Uncommon Cormorant* is the blank map of Ireland which Rob the Robot Car draws on the ground whenever the characters wish to travel from one place to another; its very blankness seems so suggestive of possibility while also emphasising Ireland's status as an island. In *Literature, Partition and the Nation State* Cleary outlines how culture can be used either to consolidate or to challenge partitionist identities and, in the case of Ireland, he emphasises the significance for nationalists of its status as an island. He points out that, while logo maps of the Republic usually represent the island as a whole, logo maps of Northern Ireland usually represent the six-county state as if it were a separate island altogether. Whether the blank map of Ireland is an aspirational image of unity for O'Hara is debatable; her integration of the capital, the Gaeltacht and the northern state certainly seems suggestive of a more inclusive imagining of Ireland.

Traditional Unionist fears that an independent united Ireland would inevitably constitute a Catholic theocracy are reflected in *The Hiring Fair* in Willie Stewarts's comments regarding the role of the Catholic Church in the rise and fall of Parnell. That the legal right to divorce was still a matter of debate in the Republic at the time of publication in 1993 lent contemporary resonance, raising questions about the separation of church and state which illuminate the Unionist point of view. Sectarian tension is explored in *The Hiring Fair* through the initial distrust apparent between the Catholic girls and their Protestant employers. However, the girls' fears never materialise and mutual respect is finally established. The Revival ideal of unity of culture transcending political and sectarian divisions is evident in both *Blaeberry Sunday* and *Penny-farthing Sally*, in which friendships occur between Protestants and Catholics through a joint interest in Gaelic culture.

The comic potential of the many ironies of the Revival is not lost on O'Hara. The overwrought enthusiasm of Miss Bannister ('the Visitor') for the Irish language (and all things native) combined with her lack of proficiency in it make for comic moments in *Blaeberry Sunday,* perhaps none so entertaining as her initial meeting with Sally's granny on arrival at the Gallagher homestead. 'Who in the name of God is that creature? ... She looks like a Protestant sort of a one to me' exclaims Granny at the sight of the uncomprehending but fascinated Visitor, who asks permission to 'take a peep' at Granny in her bed as at some exotic native specimen. Miss Bannister's idealisation of Glenbra, together with her oblique references to 'the savages' in 'the jungles of Africa', reflects a fascination with exotic otherness such as Edward Said (1978) has argued is endemic to the imperial mindset, and often in turn replicated in nationalist discourse. That such fascination verges on voyeurism is forcibly brought home by O'Hara's portrayal of the bizarre theatricality of the eviction of a young widow, dehumanised by curious onlookers.

Declan Kiberd suggests that 'the very construction of a Gaeltacht, a zone of pristine nativism, might itself be an effect of colonialism rather than an obvious answer to it' (Kiberd 1996). O'Hara's deconstruction of the Gaeltacht, through her ironic depiction of the nativist elements of Revivalist thinking, establishes it as normal rather than exceptional. Indeed, in the eyes of the people of Glenbra, it is the Visitor who is the curiosity. Though writing in English, O'Hara, like Eilís Dillon before her, gives us to understand that Irish is the spoken language of the Glenbra community. The Irish language is normalised, portrayed as a living, viable vernacular, albeit in the past, to young readers of today, most of whom know it only as a subject taught in school. Through the figure of Sally, who is equally proficient in both Irish and English, O'Hara invokes the ideal of bilingualism espoused, but never actually achieved, by the Republic. In her close engagement with Irish literature in both languages, Sally straddles the Irish Ireland/Anglo-Irish divide described by DP Moran in his influential article 'The Battle of Two Civilisations', published in the *New Ireland Review* in August 1900. Douglas Hyde's *Casadh an tSugáin* and Yeats's first play *The Countess Cathleen* both feature. (The Yeats play actually described, however, and which Sally finds so inspirational, is in fact his later play *Cathleen Ni Houlihan*, which was not staged until 1902, three years after that in which the novel is set. Equally, the *Playboy of the Western World* riots, mentioned by Mrs Erikson, did not occur until 1907. The trilogy is otherwise well researched, as well as being beautifully written.)

PJ Matthews posits 1899 (the year in which *Penny-farthing Sally* is set) as hugely significant, not only in Irish cultural history but also in the development of Irish politics (Matthews 2003). It was a year that saw the inaugural production of the Irish Literary Theatre and the emergence of a new separatist nationalism generated by the outbreak of the Boer War. In recreating such seminal events through the eyes of her heroine and in evoking the intensity of the public debates they generated, O'Hara brings to life, at a politically significant time in the 1990s, a key moment in the history of Ireland's decolonisation. The rise of nationalism, the emergence of a national literature and the transition to modernity are wonderfully evoked by O'Hara for young readers of the 1990s also living at a time of national regeneration and rapid modernisation.

Disillusionment with the 'Celtic tiger' of the new millennium is apparent in O'Hara's recent novels, *The Sparkling Rain* and *Hurlamaboc*, both set in Dublin and aimed at a teenage readership. The ugly, reductive, suburban Dublin of *The Sparkling Rain* falls far short of the regenerated society imagined by Revivalists and invoked so inspirationally by O'Hara in *Penny-farthing Sally*. After the imprisonment of their father and the death of their somewhat negligent mother, Clara and her brothers are forced to leave their beloved home in rural France to live with their scheming Irish relatives in the aptly named Grey Walls in Dublin, where Clara must play poor relation to her spoilt, fat cousin Monica (reminiscent of Dudley in the Harry Potter novels). Inspired by legend, Clara summons an inner magic to mastermind the children's escape back to France. The blend of realism with the magic of legend, which is a hallmark of O'Hara's writing, is again in evidence, as is a richly evocative use of intertextuality. Twenty-first century Ireland is ultimately rejected in this novel and portrayed as embodying a squalid materialism and mediocrity similar to that denounced by Yeats in 'September 1913'. In some ways a departure for O'Hara, *The Sparkling Rain* depicts a harsher reality, where the self-reliance of the young is necessary because of the failure of the adults in their world, a theme also evident in *Hurlamaboc*. Clara must make her own meaning of experience, a responsibility that is challenging and confusing but ultimately empowering and liberating. Storying is central to this meaning-making process and the leather-bound troubadour's book in which Clara writes her story takes on an almost magical significance.

The Sparkling Rain is also, however, a return to an earlier motif. It is, like *Hugo and the Sunshine Girl*, a variant on the legend 'The Maiden as Helper in the Hero's Flight'. This time, however, the overwhelming emphasis is on female agency and self-realisation. While the swan metaphor is perhaps somewhat strained at times and the children's flight in a stolen plane from Ireland to France requires considerable suspension of disbelief on the reader's part, *The Sparkling Rain* is a literary novel which, in beautifully evoking the complex interior life of the heroine, raises questions about the meaning of life and of love.

O'Hara's most recent novel, *Hurlamaboc*, for which she reverted to her original name, is, unusually, a coming-of-age, urban teenage novel in the Irish language. What is particularly interesting is Ní Dhuibhne's distinctive rendering of the language. Having given us to believe that Irish is the spoken language of the Glenbra community in *Blaeberry Sunday*, Ní Dhuibhne now, through the medium of the Irish language, evokes the spoken English of south Dublin teenagers. Her distinctively English rendering of the Irish language is an interesting inversion of the Irish rendering of English which characterises many of the masterpieces of the Literary Revival. The Ireland portrayed here, however, is less than heroic. Ascaill na Fuinseoige, the wealthy suburban area in which both Emma and Ruán live, has echoes of Wisteria Lane; its fashionable residents, with their luxurious detached houses and perfectly landscaped gardens, are, by and large, shallow, materialistic and morally complacent. Romantic

Ireland appears to be truly dead and gone. Emma's father, whom she sees at weekends, is a poet whose choice to write in the Irish language prevents him from achieving material success. His idealism distinguishes him from the novel's other adult characters and appears to have influenced Emma, who is interested in languages and literature and has aspirations to be a writer herself. That O'Hara chooses to write in Irish for a teenage readership is significant. Perhaps in a truly multicultural Ireland the Irish language will enjoy a status never really attained in a supposedly bilingual republic.

In an article entitled 'The Writer Writes', O'Hara (1996) refers to the novel *Sophie's Choice*, in which the heroine learns to ask the basic philosophical questions: Why are we here? Where did we come from? Where did the world come from? Her own is a thought-provoking and questioning fiction, which explores the quest for meaning that is at the centre of each individual's journey towards self-realisation. It also raises questions about the meaning of Irish national identity in today's world. Significantly, it emphasises the importance of imaginative vision to both.

References

Cleary, Joe (2002) *Literature, Partition and the Nation State* Cambridge University Press

Gregory, Lady Augusta (1902, republished 1970) *Cuchulainn of Muirthemne* Gerrards Cross: Colin Smythe (originally published by John Murray)

Kiberd, Declan (1996) *Inventing Ireland: The Literature of the Modern Nation* London: Vintage

Matthews, PJ (2003) *Revival: The Abbey Theatre, Sinn Féin, the Gaelic League and the Cooperative Movement* Cork: Cork University Press

Moran, DP (1900, republished in 1990) 'The Battle of Two Civilisations' in Seamus Deane (ed) *Field Day Anthology of Irish Writing* Derry: Field Day Publications (vol. 2)

Ní Dhuibhne, Éilís (1990) 'Liberation Fun, Truancy and Subversion' *Children's Books in Ireland* (December)

O'Hara, Elizabeth (1996) 'The Writer Writes' *Children's Books in Ireland* (May)

Said, Edward (1978/1991) *Orientalism: Western Concepts of the Orient* London: Penguin

Mark O'Sullivan

By AJ Piesse

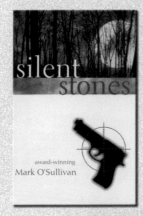

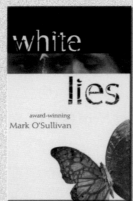

Titles by Mark O'Sullivan

Silent Stones (1999) Wolfhound

Wash-Basin Street Blues (1998) Wolfhound

White Lies (1997) Wolfhound

Angels without Wings (1997) Wolfhound

More than a Match (1996) Wolfhound

Melody for Nora (1994) Wolfhound

Mark O'Sullivan

By AJ Piesse

Reading chronologically through Mark O'Sullivan's six novels, there's a striking sense, with the nearly perfect *Silent Stones*, of arriving back at the point of departure with a renascent sense of what it is that's being seen and represented. O'Sullivan, with six novels in seven years and a plethora of awards and recommendations to his credit, was clearly one of the main players in the recent renaissance in Irish children's writing. Oddly, though an ordered reading of the texts clearly demonstrates an inexorable strengthening of writerly skill and an increasingly intricate intellectualism, the most decisive of those awards attached to the first book, *Melody for Nora*.

While *Melody For Nora* demonstrates, in principle at least, one of the foundations on which the later books will be built – that is, the creation of a realistic, uncompromising, exasperatingly stroppy central character, with an older, wearily-wiser, life-battered no-hoper as a foil – the technicalities of the writing show little promise of what is to come. Both *Melody for Nora* and its sequel, *Wash-Basin Street Blues*, are essentially flawed by the mismatch between the robust, realistic language of their characters and the paraphernalia that attaches to the *mise-en-scène* of that language. Rather than trusting his dialogue to work for itself (which it is perfectly capable of doing), O'Sullivan seems compelled to explain himself as he goes along, as the following exchange between Nora and Alec will demonstrate:

> 'If I offended you…' he started but she told him it was all right. She didn't have time to be petulant.
>
> As he went about unwrapping and tightening her bandages his gloved hands trembled and he apologised again and again for his clumsiness.
>
> 'Had a few too many last night, I'm afraid,' he laughed unconvincingly.

This stirred her once more and she suddenly felt less sorry for him than she had allowed herself to moments before.

'Why do you do things like that? Don't you know all the trouble it causes?' she snapped.

'I'm doing no harm to anyone only myself,' he said.

'What about your parents or your wife and children?'

'I'm not married and my mother and father gave up on me long ago.'

She knew she'd already said too much but it was difficult not to go on.

A similar – and potentially a much more serious – problem arises in *More Than a Match,* where the protagonist Lida Hendel's self-loathing attaches itself to her perception of her German ancestry. Her (ultimately misplaced) self-directed racism is at once so strong and so dislocated from any kind of counterbalance or contradictory interior voice that it occasionally seems to be blatant racism on the author's, rather than the character's, part (witness Lida's exchange with Mrs Mackey on page 38).

While the text generally has moments of real insight and beauty (for example, when Rose Stannix, succumbing to the inarticulate persuasion of Tommy's piano playing, drifts Miss Havisham-like downstairs to dance her redemptive foxtrot with Hubert), this lack of consistency in the tenor of the writing destabilises the medium of the text to such a degree that a smooth communication of its message is seriously jeopardised. At the same time, though, this book is another example of O'Sullivan's ability to be uncompromising in his representation of character: his heroines are bolshy, his heroes apathetic, all are essentially, realistically flawed, creating a lot of useful work for the reader by unsettling any sense of authorial dictatorship. People are complicated, difficult things, and this author is not going to tell his readers what's right and what's wrong with them. In the early texts, then, the author utterly refuses to write down to his readership in terms of his characters, but seems unable to resist compensating for this stylistically.

Each of these earlier texts has a carefully constructed plot over which exciting, suspense-driven narratives unfold, and O'Sullivan is equally uncompromising here in his drive towards an honest resolution that studiously avoids bathos. The problem with each of the three in turn is simply that of the narratorial framework out of which the characters speak.

In *Angels Without Wings*, O'Sullivan finds an astonishing solution to these awkwardnesses. He confronts the process of writing head-on, by constructing a highly complex framework that investigates both the question of the source of the narrative voice and the issue of authorial self-censorship in terms of political correctness. This highly sophisticated book reveals layers within layers. O'Sullivan confronts the reader with text as social manipulation, beginning with the burning of books in Nazi Germany, and allowing that most innocuous of genres, the children's adventure story, to take a place of equal importance among the writings of Freud, Mann, Zweig and Hesse.

In this book, poet-turned children's-writer Axel Hoffen is required by the Nazi regime to engineer his adventure stories to encourage pro-Aryan behaviour. He refuses, and a politically controlled ghost writer, Gott, is brought in to write the texts in his name. In this fashion O'Sullivan is able to demonstrate a variety of authorial voices and registers while clearly distancing himself, as author proper, from the political tenor of part of the text.

By showing the characters within Hoffen and Gott's episodes as near-helpless pawns in the political manipulation of Germany's youth, O'Sullivan simultaneously creates explicit experimental authorial voices that are protected by the overarching narrative of his own text, and creates an all-embracing metaphor concerning the relationship between characters within literature and ourselves as actors in life's narrative. One by one, Hoffen's child protagonists become aware of the texts they are being written into – that is, they wake up to the texts-within-the-text and struggle against the new roles being inscribed upon them, strenuously exerting their innate personalities against Gott's manipulations.

That the characters begin to take on a life of their own and become able to act physically within O'Sullivan's implied real world is part of the extended allegory that is hinted at in the naming of the adult protagonists – Teufel (devil) the stormtrooper; Hoffen (hope) the poet and creator of the original, innocuous Lingen gang; and (rather worryingly) Gott (God) the ghostwriter who has become a dissolute drunk and, like Hoffen (and indeed Teufel), dies before the book is finished.

The members of the gang supersede the fictional texts-within-the-text and step out into the real world of O'Sullivan's text, making clear the author's ultimate point that literature has a real and tangible effect on the real world. As if that weren't complex enough, O'Sullivan's readers are left dallying, tantalisingly, with the notion that Axel Hoffen is for real, is a real poet of Nazi Germany, and the text that he or she is holding and reading was 'discovered' years after the war. The appendix, containing Hoffen's prison poems, continues the textual game-playing up until the very last moment.

By drawing attention to the very processes of writing and making clear distinctions between the pseudo-real and pseudo-fictional sections, O'Sullivan forces the reader to make value judgements about style, about validity of character, about the role and responsibility of the writer, about the essential nature of the fictional text, and about the role of the reader as participator in creation of meaning. In working out these complex relations, the reader is also set the puzzle of the huge metaphysical questions being asked here too: if hope (Hoffen) gives up, rediscovers itself and is then slaughtered, if God (Gott) is a maudlin old drunk in the pay of a fascist regime whose final act of courage is to give his creations the option of creating their own futures out of a set of notes, what will drive these creations when they cease to be authored? The detective story within the novel is, among other things, a mechanism for O'Sullivan to raise questions about text, authorship, character, while allowing him to use a series of registers and scenarios. Ultimately, the episodes actually become experiments in degrees of register and style.

In *White Lies*, O'Sullivan narrows down the range of experimentation. Choosing a less complex form, he allows his characters this time to step free of an authorially driven framework by presenting alternating chapters of first-person direct address. Freeing the wonderfully authentic voices of Nance and OD from the 'he-said, she-said' constrictions of his earlier books, O'Sullivan subtly encourages the reader to puzzle out, alongside the two main protagonists, exactly what is going on in their heads and to experience the gradual articulation of situations alongside them. The immediacy and interiority of these voices can be breathtakingly simple, for example, this moment of sharing impossibly slowly passing time with Nance: 'I kept telling myself not to look at my watch, and I kept looking at it. Nine, quarter past, twenty past, twenty-two minutes past.'

Each of the four main characters has a problematic relationship with their parents, with arriving at a comfortable version of themselves to live with and to show the world, and with articulating those difficulties either to themselves or among their families and confidants. By using first-person direct address, and by allowing Nance and OD to comment on the same incidents from different points of view, O'Sullivan is able to hold back from giving full explanations and to give the impression that the text is free of any kind of manipulation. The dividend for this restraint is a highly convincing reconstruction of two minds tacitly, frustratedly acknowledging their own lack of omniscience. Early in the book, for example, Nance finds a photograph that suggests that her adoptive parents (one of whom is the deputy principal of her community college) have been lying to her about her background. Unable to articulate her anxiety, she argues with OD, and then, inexplicably, without premeditation,

> I opened the geography book I'd been studying before he'd called. OD had given it to me when he'd walked out of school. His initials were still on the front cover.
>
> I flicked through the pages. I got to the chapter on Africa and my finger slowly followed the outline of that continent until it came to Kenya. I tore out the page with venom, crumpled it up and threw it in the fire. I did the same with every other page in the book. Then I ripped the cover to pieces and watched as the flames encircled the initials, 'OD', and swallowed them up, and the frail black remains fell asunder among the red-hot coals.
>
> The Maths book came next…

The evocation of the hypnotic stare into the fire as the hands mechanically continue the process of destruction and the recording of the half-completed thoughts about what's happening show the extent to which O'Sullivan is able to handle these new interior voices.

Silent Stones returns to a more traditional format, but by now O'Sullivan is adept at producing authentic voices for his characters and at conveying an apparently self-driven plot. There is scarcely a spare word in the text. Dialogue is so carefully crafted that many of the acts of speech in the text are left freestanding: what is said contains within itself the way in which it is said. The similarities between Mayfly and Robby dealing with the potential loss of a mother, being caught up in a mode of living that is historically imposed on them, unable to understand what drives their father's political stance, given its consequences are not blatantly parallel, but occasionally coincide, so that these structural balances are felt rather than perceived directly. There's an ability to move between internal voice and external observation without always signalling the shift by change of font or announcing a separate voice in any other fashion.

Returning to the notion of how war destroys families, and how even the wholehearted embracing of peace will not necessarily save a life, O'Sullivan's newly honed style is more than a match for the subtlety of his argument here. It is as if the canon of his writing is an explicit demonstration of the steps an author might go through to achieve this synthesis of form and content. Having been taken on a tour of the material concepts in the early texts, we have been invited to watch the processes of construction in the middle two, and are now presented with a completed edifice, fully aware of the tensions that hold it up, but more bowled over by its beauty than its bricks and mortar. The gentle authorial intrusions in this text are integrated by virtue of their consistency of tone with the characters' register, and as the book begins its conclusion, about three-quarters of the way through, one moment of description is perhaps O'Sullivan tacitly acknowledging his own achievement in this latest raid on inarticulacy:

> In the end, it was the tone of their voices, their harmony, that mattered, not the stories they had to tell. Their fears and uncertainties didn't miraculously resolve themselves; but sharing them with each other was an answer in itself.

Siobhán Parkinson

By AJ Piesse

Selected titles by Siobhán Parkinson

Blue Like Friday (2007) Puffin

Something Invisible (2006) Puffin

Second Fiddle or How to Tell a Blackbird from a Sausage (2005) Puffin

The Love Bean (2002) O'Brien

Animals Don't Have Ghosts (2002) O'Brien

Cows are Vegetarians (2001) O'Brien

Call of the Whales (2000) O'Brien

Breaking the Wishbone (1999) O'Brien

The Moon King (1998) O'Brien

Four Kids, Three Cats, Two Cows, One Witch (Maybe) (1997) O'Brien

Sisters ... No Way! (1996) O'Brien 1996

All Shining in the Spring: The Story of a Baby who Died (1995) O'Brien

No Peace for Amelia (1994) O'Brien

Amelia (1993) O'Brien

The Dublin Adventure (1992) O'Brien

The Country Adventure (1992) O'Brien

Siobhán Parkinson

By AJ Piesse

Irish writing for children experienced an undeniable stretching of the limbs during the last decades of the 20th century. Children's writers in Ireland responded to unprecedented exponential economic and social change with a newly robust and resonant literature for an increasingly sophisticated cosmopolitan and diverse young readership.

Siobhán Parkinson's novels, and her occasional acerbic outbursts in the press, were among the first to epitomise the alertness and intelligence of the new awareness of and writing for young people in Ireland, and her career has been distinguished by the way in which her writing has kept pace with the growth in sophistication of her readership. What Pat Donlon (1999) has described as her 'ironic and laconic view of life' is in evidence in the dry wit of *The Dublin Adventure* and *The Country Adventure*; and her commitment to the intellectual capabilities of quite young children is evident in her later rewriting of both pieces (as *Animals Don't Have Ghosts* and *Cows are Vegetarians*, respectively) in the first person.

Her clear-eyed account of the death of a newborn infant in *All Shining in the Spring: The Story of a Baby who Died* is as much a tribute to the emotional capabilities of the very young as it is the epitome of poetic economy, both demonstrated in the title itself. The short sentences and simple statements throw into relief the deeply moving moments of direct speech, ('"He's only a baby," said Matthew sadly to his mother. "He didn't even have a chance to see you"') providing an austere articulation of the complexity of feeling beneath the surface of the prose.

In the early companion novels *Amelia* and *No Peace for Amelia*, Parkinson creates a double diptych. The broad movement from the first to the second is from innocence to experience, while the compared and contrasted world views of the two central protagonists check and balance each other continually across both novels. Amelia, initially the complacent, middle-class, much-loved daughter of a highly successful merchant father and a politically progressive (if somewhat dotty) mother (think Mrs Banks in the film version of *Mary Poppins*), is in stark opposition to sharp-tongued, sharp-witted Mary-Anne, the no-nonsense maid-of-all-work.

The collapse of Amelia's father's business forces a reassessment of hitherto unquestioned beliefs. Uncompromisingly, Parkinson confronts Amelia, and the reader, with new angles on quotidian commonplaces. Parkinson's trademark ability to convey the child protagonist's innate comprehension fettered by incomplete articulation is spontaneously generated by the day-to-day narrative of *Amelia*, the mundane featly interwoven with the momentous.

As Pádraic Whyte (2006) has pointed out, Parkinson is using certain elements of child psychology both 'as a mode of writing and as a method of analysis to explore both the development of a character and the cultural history of a nation'. Her unerring ability to capture outward detail in a few deft sketches carries the dualities within these novels to a structural level too. The outward descriptions, as in real life, are fully fashioned, but the authorial rendition of the inner knowledge being attained by the characters is, crucially and cannily, often allowed to remain incomplete.

The structural notion of the double-take reaches its apogee in the award-winning *Sisters … No Way!* which consists of two first-person accounts of the same story. The novel has two front covers, designed so that the reader has no clue which account to read first, or to which to give precedence. The contrasting idiolects, Ashling's maternally mundane and materialistic, Cindy's laced with literary reference and unapologetic arrogance, each irritate the reader with splendid impartiality. The deficits of character revealed by each narrator's account are checked and balanced by the alternative point of view.

But again, this novel is more than the sum of two parts. The names of Cindy and Ashling, the acquisition of a step-parent by each protagonist, and the handsome young stranger bringing a lost shoe to the home of the fleet-at-midnight object of his desire all invite the reader to think again and think harder. Barely credible at times, tedious Ashling and over-studied, self-dramatising Cindy teeter on the brink of caricature. Life is not a fairy tale, but if Doc Martens can be allowed to replace glass slippers (and bunny slippers to replace Doc Martens) then the reader will learn to discriminate between intelligent reading and over-reading. Less ostensibly, the over-hasty marriage hard on the heels of Cindy's mother's death, the funeral baked meats coldly furnishing forth the wedding tables and driving Cindy into black-clad self-contemplation, the perverse redemptive aunt, all suggest (to this reader anyway) that Parkinson has more than one prince in mind. We might think that we construct our own narratives, our own accounts of our own lives, Parkinson seems to be saying, but there is always someone else writing their version of us, and, furthermore, there is no escaping what Harold Bloom has called the 'anxiety of influence', the fact that there is no narrative new under the sun, that if we do write a narrative of self, it will inevitably be read in terms of narratives that already exist.

Considered by many to be her best novel, *Four Kids, Three Cats, Two Cows, One Witch (Maybe)* is witty in all its aspects. Replete with Blytonesque picnic (lost, on this occasion), snobbery (here regretted, eventually, and overcome) and obligatory odd adult to replace absent parents, the novel transcends its form by showing the protagonists rewriting themselves by telling their own stories. The peculiar Irishness of island writing too is invoked here: the intricacies of Eilís Dillon's masterly exploration of insularity in all its forms in *The Island of Ghosts* (1990) are recalled, and the realignment of fantasy and reality at the moment of the thunderstorm (replete this time, through its annexation to a sensitive portrait of bewildered but ferocious old age, weakness of mind and howling against the elements of modern life, with allusions to *Lear*) finds resonance in the Irish children's canon too, strongly recalling Patricia Lynch's evocation of the narrow boundaries between degrees of fantasy in, say, the later chapters of *The Turf-Cutter's Donkey* (1934).

But the shift in register required to understand the function of the struc-ture of this novel aligns the ideas more closely with adult writing like

Jeanette Winterson's – 'Listen. I'm telling you stories' in *Oranges Are Not the Only Fruit* (1985) – or Allende's short stories. The real cleverness of this novel subsists in the risks Parkinson takes by, for example, making some of the most revealing moments the funniest – as when Dympna draws attention to the functionality of naming. Dympna says that her cow is called Dympna; Beverley says 'Really? Isn't that confusing?' and Dympna replies, 'No, I don't think so. I call her Dympna. She doesn't call me anything.'

Boundaries are continually called into question: those between fantasy and reality, between fact and fiction, between madness and sanity, between articulation and communication. The metatextual message, as usual, is that the story itself will yield up the reason why it is so and no other way.

In *The Moon King*, in my view probably still the best of the novels, Parkinson revisits the notion of inarticulateness, and the understated, powerful simplicity of *All Shining in the Spring* re-emerges in a newly robust form. Young Ricky's abused, damaged personality, which manifests itself psychologically by traumatised silence, is rendered brilliantly by a fragmented interior monologue, usually preceded by a slightly fuller account from a third-person narrative that is already shifting towards Ricky's own idiolect. This treatment of speech imitates a general motif in the novel, that of degrees of anxiety. The foster family Parkinson creates is not a perfect safe world, and other characters are troubled too. It is never quite clear which children are fostered and which are birth-family. Ricky's trauma is placed in the context of degrees of trauma, his erratic behaviour one particular form of several forms. The shifting in and out of register to produce Ricky's voice is a particular form of this nuancing, and it brings the preoccupation home powerfully. Ricky's inarticulacy can be described by the narrator/grasped by the reader if it's described in regular language; the narrator can represent it partly through a shift to narrated stream-of-consciousness; but the isolation his damaged world-view imposes on him can only be felt by letting him speak internally to himself, in still more fragmented speech, in a typeface that alienates it from the rest of the text.

Breaking the Wishbone demonstrates a similarly accurate ear for idiolect. Parkinson's experiment in direct speech with an extreme sparseness of detail is a departure from her usually vivid description, but the voices bring the characters and their surroundings starkly to life. Most poignant here are the occasional flashes of humour, the juxtapositions of despair and desperate attempts at some kind of normality, of 'gaiety transfiguring all that dread'. In repatterning her writing to her purpose, Parkinson takes the risk of freeing the characters from being reported; yet again, it is in telling their own stories that they are able to take control, to a limited degree, of their own futures.

Call of the Whales is the closest Parkinson has yet come to a crossover book. The marvellous sense of nostalgia, the evocation of what she has elsewhere called 'forgotten, joyous corners of the imagination' (Parkinson 1999) dominates the yearning to reconnect with the narrator's own past and sense of wonder. The circularity of experience is caught fleetingly with an Eliotesque recapitulation at the end of the novel. Again, the notions of coming of age in an alien place, the necessity of understanding and accepting alternative points of view, the simultaneous pull towards home and towards a new and independent self, form an unobtrusive undercurrent to the breathtakingly elegant narrative stream. With this novel, the traumas of adolescence are a matter for reflection, not for immediate experience, and the settled nature of the form in which she writes underscores the notion of recollection in tranquillity.

In *The Love Bean*, Parkinson meets the changing face of Irish ethnic diversity head-on. The novel is a multiple investigation of similarity and differentiation. Two sets of twins, at two highly distinct periods in Irish history, are brought face to face with the tensions between unique identity and twinship. For each set of twins, the catalyst for the differentiation process is the arrival of an attractive young man completely alien to the twins' culture: in one case, a young Roman, in the other, an African asylum seeker. Universal issues of identity – those of race, culture and gender stereotype – align themselves in parallel against those of individual differentiation. All this (and there are two witty, engaging, exciting story-lines to hold it all together) is set within a framework of quotation from *Romeo and Juliet*. From within, the novel is held together by the notion of passing on a love-gift across gender, generational and cultural divides.

The issues are timely, immensely thought-provoking and sensitively but insistently addressed. Previous ideas of doubling, of intertextuality, of time present being bound up in time past are revisited, but at the same time, Irishness at its most ancient and at its most present is shown to have the same personal and universal preoccupations: individuality, insularity, tensions between generations and social groups and between expectation and resignation. There is a sense here, not just of stories informing each other, but of the very narrative of history informing and reforming itself.

Parkinson draws attention again and again to the question of what makes us who we are, where we find the language of the self, what things make us simultaneously different and the same.

Her 2005 novel, *Second Fiddle or How to Tell a Blackbird from a Sausage* is set up as a fiction within a fiction, the reader being told early on by narrator Mags that although there are two first-person voices, both are created by Mags. This narrator occasionally offers helpful notes on reading the text, urging the reader to be aware of and critical of 'authorial' practice ('I don't think Gillian would be capable of constructing this sentence, actually, but I have to give her adult-sounding things to say from time to time, because she is a bit older than I am') and draws attention to unresolved plot details at the end, inviting readers to consider what has been left unsaid as well as directing conscious attention to the rhetoric of narrative practice. In this very prickly account of the struggle towards autonomy, Parkinson rewards the thoughtful reader with the realisation that direct address from a narrator does not necessarily result in absolute transparency, and the refusal to provide tidy resolution to conflicting interests that dominates the text is epitomised in two deliberately provocative comments towards the very end of the novel. 'You never do know anything really about anything, until after it has happened, and even then you don't know much either, which is why life is so confusing and why books are usually better than life, because in books it is the author's job to make things less confusing for the reader' observes Mags in the closing stages, causing the reader to reflect immediately that the author of this text (Parkinson) seems to have gone out of her way to point out precisely how complex life, and the narration of life, actually is. The final sentence is in itself a tacit acceptance that the text is a three-way negotiation among author, narrator and reader: 'I think that is everything, except for Grandpa, who is the same as ever. He says isn't it just as well that he didn't move in with us because now look, whatever that is supposed to mean'.

The same kind of self-conscious reflection drives *Something Invisible* and *Blue Like Friday*. In each of these texts, the interior voice of the central character is generally at odds with the perceptions of the other characters around them, so that the reflexivity of the text is more implicitly bound up in the character than explicitly expressed in the form. In *Something Invisible*, the three opening chapters, with a single sentence each, act out little in the way in which Parkinson will evoke protagonist Jake's partial perception and articulation of the events that befall him.

Unobtrusively crafted parallels drive the novel: Jake saves an unknown child from drowning, thinking he is diving in to save his friend's small sister Joanne, and is then accidentally instrumental in the death of the same child later in the book, unable to leap to her rescue when she runs behind her mother's reversing car to greet him because he is carrying his own new baby sister in a sling. The birth of his sister Daisy, rather than bringing about a sense of augmentation of family and of his own role in life by becoming a big brother, brings instead a sense of diminution because it causes him to worry about whether his stepfather feels the same degree of attachment to him, Jake, as he does to his new birth-daughter, Daisy. The parallels are there at a conceptual level too, Jake's love of everything to do with fish and water manifesting itself as a desire to be a painter of fish – to be involved with these most erratic and evanescent of creatures as something beautiful, creatable, controllable – being in stark contrast to the panic he feels when practical Stella invites him for a morning's fishing with four of her small siblings in tow, his preoccupation with the understanding of colour necessary to such a career manifesting itself as a desire to have a precise and fixed name for every colour under the sun.

Fundamentally, the text deals with the relationship between knowledge and understanding, with a pre-adolescent coming to terms with complexity of feeling, shifting circumstances and learning to live with events that are beyond rational control. The novel contains some of Parkinson's best writing, I think, both in terms of subtlety and authenticity of voice, but also in the way in which the reader is allowed to grow into articulate understanding only at the same rate as Jake. For example, the idiolectical tone of the narrative (introduced from the beginning with 'he found they generally acted superior', a spoken tone investing personality in a reported voice) only speaks of 'Jake's dad' until Jake suffers his crisis of belonging on the birth of his sister, the reader is as disturbed by the sudden recognition of the idea of 'Dad' actually being 'stepfather' as Jake is himself. It's this degree of subtlety, this degree of tacit alignment with the protagonist's point of view that intensifies so dramatically the reader's mutual experience of the moment when

> the shiny back bumper of the pretty car clipped the child sideways on at speed, and Joanne's little body flew sideways into the air, all flailing limbs, like a cat that has missed its footing in an upwards leap, the long stick whipped out of her hand, turning and turning, like the only visible spoke in an invisible wheel. The little girl seemed almost to float to the ground and landed soundlessly in the middle of the road, like a fallen star, all akimbo, utterly still. The stick rolled away on the camber of the road, into the gutter.

I quote at length here because the manipulation of shared point-of-view is masterly, shifting from admiration of the car ('shiny', 'pretty') and recognition of real-time speed ('clipped', 'at speed') to the suspended time and defamiliarisation ('the only visible spoke in an invisible wheel') that gives us a crucial few seconds for assimilation and self-protection at such moments of extreme emotional stress. Internal alliteration redoubles and finally endstops the phrases in apposition, which mimic movement moving to stillness in the ever-shortening rhythm of 'like a fallen star, all akimbo, utterly still'. We are even granted a few more seconds out from the moment when we will have to confront the consequences of the incident by being allowed to look away, momentarily, from the body as 'the stick rolled away on the camber of the road, into the gutter'. Parkinson conjures intensity in the briefest of observations in this text: 'The summer felt old' begins the last chapter, transferred epithet and oxymoron working simultaneously to produce a real desolation. While the storyline pulls no punches at all, Jake being mercilessly dragged from a morass of self-pity by a kindly but briskly pitiless older neighbour, the sheer beauty of the writing pulls the reader back repeatedly to the text, provoking precisely the reflection on response that Jake has to learn amid the chaos of the events recounted.

Parkinson's 2007 novel, *Blue Like Friday*, also considers the choices young people have to make about ways of being. Protagonist Hal has only two memories of his dead father, one of which, flying a kite with him, will become a metaphor for release, reconciliation and celebration of what little time they had together. The other is a memory of deeply polished chestnut brown shoes at five-year-old eye level, Hal's abiding memory of finding his father dead. Hal can't imagine why he should remember the shoes, but his preoccupation with synaesthesia, which mostly manifests itself as identifying everything with a colour and also knowing how that colour tastes and smells, suggests a tendency to transfer meaning and focus, inviting an inference that Hal's memory is actually of a hanging body with deep brown shoes at eye level. The repression of the real meaning of the moment is cast into deep relief by the very explicit reaction Hal has when his mother moves her long-term boyfriend Alec into the house; most of the hilarious plot is driven by the fallout from a plan to get Alec out of favour with Hal's mother and thus out of the running as a live-in partner. There are some bold games going on in the text – it becomes apparent after a little while that the characters' names and certain details of the plot resonate with a particular Shakespeare play whose protagonist isn't too happy about his mother remarrying either – but two motifs – that of synaesthesia and the game of 'kinds' that the children continually play ('If you were a cathedral, would you be Gothic or Romanesque?') – combine to show that here, as in *Something Invisible*, the truth most often reveals itself if it is approached obliquely. In this novel more than any other to date, Parkinson privileges the reader's intelligence, setting up false analogies for those prone to over-reading both outside the text (see the Hamlet riff) and within it (the tattooing episode, and the children's reaction to Alec's apparently prolonged visit to the morgue). Hal's tendency to create a reality that's comfortable for his own habitation is shown to have been a good survival technique, but one that needs to be outgrown, and once again Parkinson's refusal to be sentimental about death and difficulty in childhood ultimately privileges the child protagonist in every way.

Since starting to publish in the early 1990s, Parkinson has been extraordinarily prolific, and the breadth of genre and variety of voice she has assimilated to the body of her work shows a highly intelligent facility with form and an uncompromising attention to the detail of her prose. Her novels are increasingly intellectually demanding, I think, increasingly confident in their evocation of register and timbre, and increasingly resonant with the preoccupations of literatures beyond those of Irish writing for children, but they rarely allow their cleverness to subordinate their proper function – that illumination of real life so that we see it all at once strange and new, and yet with a shock of recognition.

References

Donlon, Patricia (1999) 'Siobhan Parkinson' in S Prendergast and Tom Prendergast (eds) *St James Guide to Children's Writers* Detroit and London: St James Press (p 828)

Parkinson, Siobhán (1999) 'Show Some Respect' *The Irish Times* 5 October

Whyte, Pádraic (2006) 'The Construction of History and Childhood in Literature and Film for Children in Ireland 1990–2003' unpublished PhD dissertation, Trinity College, Dublin

Niamh Sharkey

By John Short

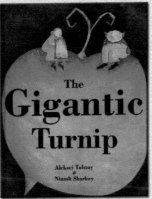

Picturebooks by Niamh Sharkey

I'm a Happy Hugglewug (2006) Walker

Santasaurus (2005) Walker

The Ravenous Beast (2003) Walker

Malachy Doyle *Tales from Old Ireland* (2000) Barefoot

Richard Walker *Jack and the Beanstalk* (1999) Barefoot

Aleksei Tolstoy (1998) *The Gigantic Turnip* Barefoot

Hugh Lupton (1998) *Tales of Wisdom and Wonder* Barefoot

Niamh Sharkey

By John Short

Several years ago, Niamh Sharkey graduated from a course I lecture on in the Dublin Institute of Technology (DIT) in visual communications, with first class honours, having specialised in illustration. She was also selected as 'Student Designer of the Year', an independent award conferred by the Society of Designers in Ireland. She had already started focusing on children's books and developing her painterly skills in her final-year projects, and she also had a good grasp of design, a very useful skill when it comes to considering the compositional layouts of children's books. She was a quiet, hard-working student, and she always loved books. 'I always had my head stuck in a book,' she has said of herself in interview. 'I was at my happiest drawing and reading.' Art students are often interested in the design of books and how they look, but Niamh had impressive literary tastes, quite unusual in students whose main interests lie in the visual arts, and she recognises this dual interest herself: 'Illustrating children's books is a chance for me to combine my two passions.' So the stage was set.

I have followed her successes with delight and admiration through the years, as she picked up the prestigious Mother Goose award in 1998, the 1999 Blue Ribbon award for her illustrations for *The Gigantic Turnip* and the Bisto Book of the Year award of 1998/9 for *Tales of Wisdom and Wonder*. She travelled the Indian subcontinent, lived for a while in Australia and illustrated *Tales of Wisdom and Wonder* at the foot of Mount Wellington in Tasmania – how cool is that? Further picturebooks have followed, as listed in the panel.

An illustrator whose work one could compare Niamh's with is the internationally known Peter Sís, who left Czechoslovakia in the 1980s, and continued illustrating children's books after moving to New York. His work

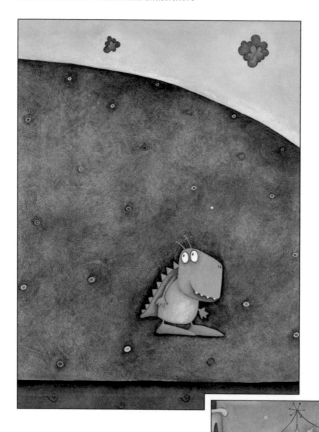

brought a new Eastern European flavour to western readers and viewers. He employed a traditional painterly technique of working meticulously on boards and prepared surfaces with oil and acrylic paints, using under-painting and glazes. He creates beautiful, timeless, atmospheric worlds reminiscent of the renaissance, but well suited also to what he does so well: the retelling of traditional folktales and stories in a new and timeless way.

Another amazingly original American illustrator, Lane Smith, who emerged in the late 1980s, has influenced a generation of illustrators, including Niamh Sharkey, and he continues to influence illustration students these days with his ground-breaking books, notably *The True Story of the Three Little Pigs* (Puffin 1989) and *The Stinky Cheese Man and Other Fairly Stupid Tales* (Puffin 1992). Lane Smith's books are anarchic and quirky and they combine a revisionist retelling of classic tales with a similarly quirky approach to the typography and overall design. He gives new twists to his exquisite painting with the added application of collage. The effect of his work is achieved through the brilliant combination of all of these elements.

Niamh's professed admiration is for another acclaimed American illus-trator, Maurice Sendak. He also spent his childhood with his 'head stuck in books', and he speaks of his 'weird geographies and creatures'. Similarly, when asked in a recent interview if she had a dream project that she would like to develop in the future, Niamh replied that she has been influenced by travelling: '… the colours and places and people that I met are stored away in my memory. I expect that many of them will pop up in my paintings in the future.'

Both Lane Smith and Peter Sís work in variations of traditional painting techniques. Many illustrators of the past and of today employ these methods, but they are pretty good examples of practitioners in this field. The laying-down of primers for paint/glaze textures and base-coat colours to instantly provide a general overall warm or cold or neutral colour base can have rewarding results. The painterly techniques Niamh employs are similar: she uses layering to create depth – a technique she could explore further – while the underpainting creates a luminosity of colour, one of the most

important features of her work. The effects achieved can be tremendously evocative and atmospheric. It is clear that Niamh has absorbed some of these influences and has adopted this slow and laborious work method and made it her own.

It is a healthy sign to see an artist's work flourish and develop as their talents are brought to bear on the next project and the next. I imagine that, with her laborious technique of oil on gesso boards, Niamh must work fairly slowly, yet she manages to keep a continuity of style throughout her books, no mean feat, considering that each book project has a gestation period of about six months to a year. She is also obviously aware of the need to develop all the time.

I really like Niamh Sharkey's second book *The Gigantic Turnip*. She approaches it roughly from a similar perspective as Lane Smith might. Here we have a classic tale, quirky illustrations and also a quirky typographic touch – this book is set, as much of Lane Smith's work also is, in Bodoni typeface. The result is good, though the influence is clear. This is not ground-breaking work, but it is a really good book and truly worthy of the award. Quite an accomplishment for her second book.

The sequences of long horizons on double pages are fun and playful. She has a brilliant sense of composition and balance, and her design sense is a great asset to her work. I should also mention that I particularly like her sense of colour here. The long horizontal group of characters silhouetted against a beautifully painted sky, almost in monochrome on a double-page spread, is lovely. This is a very tasteful and effective book with subtle changes in atmosphere throughout as the drama intensifies, right up to the huge POP! as the offending turnip pops out and they all tumble down the page. This is not unlike a scene from a painting by Hieronymus Bosch, complete against a dark sky. These are two of the many successful spreads in the book.

There is a liveliness and three-dimensional quality in this book which I think are lacking in her more stylised later work.

Jack and the Beanstalk, which closely followed *The Gigantic Turnip*, is also a fine and consistent production throughout, though I find the stylisation

and articulation of the figures a bit problematic. The wee figures are sometimes a bit static, the faces seem fairly similar. This is an aspect of her work where perhaps Niamh could develop. The personalities of individuals could be brought out further and refined. It's really a question of style over substance, I feel, particularly in the recent books. I wonder if they need all the little outlines, which they didn't have in *The Gigantic Turnip*. It tends to make the illustrations flat. The painting technique is good – it's just that the overall stylisation is a bit too caricatured for my taste, and the variations on viridian green and purple as a principal basis for colour themes can be a bit repetitive.

A plus with this book is that it is a retelling by Richard Walker of the classic story with a dramatic new and shockingly unexpected ending – the giant is catapulted from the beanstalk off into outer space! Niamh's quirky style really suits this preposterous episode and does it without reverting to cartoon tackiness. There is a lovely and unusual page earlier where the 'old lady' wanders through the cold and dark castle with her candle. She is surrounded by a collage of keys. I thought these might be scanned in and overlaid in Photoshop, but apparently Niamh does not use computer applications in her work. I don't know quite how it was done, but here is a glimpse of a technique she might develop. This kind of thing only appears once, but the effect is magical. (Just as an aside, I wonder what exactly is the relationship that the 'old lady' has with the giant? Maybe I am going out on a limb here but in the original story I think she was his wife. In this version of the story she really sells him out. He is a pretty misunderstood guy?)

One title of Niamh's which I must mention as one of the most playful, mature and beautifully designed is *Tales from Old Ireland*, a collection of classic Irish folktales by Malachy Doyle, featuring refreshing new texts, pictures and design. One criticism is that, although this book is a beautiful thing, it does feel like one tale rather than a collection of different tales. The characters throughout and the colour schemes could do with an individual flavour. Maybe I am niggling a bit here at someone who has achieved great success, but here is something I think could be refined.

In a refreshing change from books whose principal themes are one way or another about vegetables or are retellings of old myths, there came in 2003 *The Ravenous Beast*. And this time the illustrator is also the author.

Niamh is fortunate that she is able to write as well as illustrate. This dual talent is not that common. Not everyone can make the transition to author/illustrator, though Mary Murphy, another DIT graduate, also both illustrates and writes (for much younger children); not only does she write and illustrate her own work, but she also writes books that are illustrated by other illustrators.

Now, not only has Niamh Sharkey written and illustrated *The Ravenous Beast* but the publisher has added a computerised version of her own calligraphy throughout, making it the complete Sharkey experience. Walker Books seem to be particularly good at bringing out the best in an artist through thoughtful art direction and editing. It's pretty effective and the assimilation of the texts intertwined with the images is liberating and even more playful than in her previous books. The overall effect is fun, and consistent with a multitude of little and large creatures. Equally *Santasaurus* and *I'm a Happy Hugglewug* are aimed at a young readership, and their appeal for this audience is indisputable.

I do miss the depth in the painting, however, which seems to have been sacrificed for the sake of the younger readership, but these are a different kind of book after all. Gone too is the ever so slightly edgy and brooding atmosphere we had in *The Gigantic Turnip*. The darkening skies have vanished.

Curiously, the back cover of *The Ravenous Beast* features all the protagonists. The figures have been silhouetted and a drop shadow has been added. This makes them look superior, I think, to the rather flat cut-outs against the white pages within the book. However, the endpapers I liked and the overall playful, quirky fun is there, and that suits the story, which is also quirky. Essentially, it's about creatures ravenously devouring buckets of other creatures, a good story which I really enjoyed. It has been animated and released on DVD and it is likely that the *Hugglewugs* will also be made into a DVD, possibly even a series. In *Santasaurus*, the story of a

dinosaur Christmas, the endpapers are again used to advantage, especially the closing ones, as we see the young dinosaurs enjoying their presents from Santasaurus.

A retelling of the Perrault version of Cinderella by Max Eilenberg is under way and here we see Niamh bringing her own Sharkey style to a well-known tale. This has involved intense research in Trinity College Dublin's manuscript and early printed books departments. Some of her motifs are, for example, based on the Book of Hours by the Limburg brothers and others and the costumes are modelled on some depicted in 16th-century French books. She says that as her children get older she is becoming more interested in illustrating for an older audience and indeed one can see her current work appealing to more sophisticated readers. There is a welcome progression in that her most recent books are bigger and plusher productions.

Some time ago, I met another former student of mine, working as a graphic designer, who told me she wanted to get into children's book illustration, and that she had been inspired by and bought all the books of an illustrator whose work she had recently discovered. It was Niamh Sharkey. So Niamh is now at the stage where she is starting to influence and inspire a new generation of illustrators. Meanwhile, though, I am sure her own work will also develop and continue to enthral and enchant us.

Matthew Sweeney

By Robert Dunbar

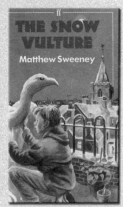

Selected titles by Matthew Sweeney

Poetry

Up on the Roof: New and Selected Poems (2001) Faber & Faber

Fatso in the Red Suit (1995) Faber & Faber

The Flying Spring Onion (1992) Faber & Faber

Novels

Fox (2002) Bloomsbury

The Snow Vulture (1992) Faber & Faber

The Chinese Dressing-Gown (1987) Raven Arts Press

Anthology (ed)

The New Faber Book of Children's Verse (2001) Faber & Faber

Adult poetry

The Bridal Suite (1997) Jonathan Cape

Matthew Sweeney

By Robert Dunbar

'There was a boy here, Mummy. I was playing with him.'

'A boy? What boy?'

'I don't know who he is.'

'Where is he, then, this boy of yours?'

'I don't know.'

– Matthew Sweeney, *The Chinese Dressing-Gown*

When Matthew Sweeney's *Up on the Roof: New and Selected Poems* was published in 2001 it should have come as no surprise that the poem chosen to open the collection was 'A Boy'. In the corpus of Sweeney's poetry for children it is the signpost poem, certainly to that substantial element of his work which focuses on his own boyhood memories and, by extension, to recurring exploration of fictional boyhoods in his three children's novels. What we are primarily concerned with in this aspect of Sweeney's work is an act of reconstruction, to which the reader is expected to contribute through speculating on the questions which Sweeney raises about memory, origins and identity.

While, stylistically, this interrogative mode characterises virtually all of Sweeney's work, it is particularly effective in his 'boyhood' poems in establishing a potent line of communication with the reader: the transition from autobiographical to generalised experience is easy and assured, assisted by a use of form which is tightly controlled and carefully structured. The initial lines of 'A Boy' set up the dualities:

Half a mile from the sea,
in a house with a dozen bedrooms

he grew up. Who was he?
Oh, nobody much. A boy
with the usual likes
and more than a few dislikes

while the final couplet succinctly and teasingly unites them:

How do I know all this?
You'd guess how if you tried.

In an article published in the May 1993 issue of *Children's Books in Ireland* Sweeney writes of how, growing up in the Donegal of the 1950s and 1960s, he became an early, avid reader, not least, perhaps, because he had an aunt who was a local librarian. 'She used,' he writes, 'to give me the keys of the library in the evenings and let me take out as many books as I wanted.' In 'A Boy' this memory is given primacy and becomes transmuted as

He got the library keys
and carried eight books at a time
home, and he read.
He read so much
he stayed in the book's world.

But there were other formative worlds also. In the same 1993 article Sweeney recalls 'the oral storytelling that was still widely practised' around his home and especially remembers his grand-uncle Owenie and friend reminiscing 'with more than a dash of fiction' about their youth. 'I was happy to sit there,' says Sweeney, 'seeing their larger-than-life, long-ago characters and their exploits take shape in my head.'

Memories real, memories fictional, the child's 'shaping' of exaggerated and colourful anecdote, often mediated in a voice testifying to their oral beginnings: these became the starting points for those poems – such as 'Singing Class', 'Cornered', 'Off School', 'The New Boy', 'Only the Walls',

'The Sleigh' and 'How We Spent Easter' – which will continue to shape recall beyond the merely fragmentary into permanent evocations of boyhood actuality and dream. But the memories are not necessarily always rosy or benign: the 'child spirits', as in the poem 'While I Practise My Piano', are sometimes 'haunting' in the uneasy sense of the adjective. The eight lines of 'Singing Class', for example, provide so taut a memoir of classroom fear and repression that the final effect is almost visceral:

> There is this image of a tuning-fork
> struck against a desk-top to loose
> its lone note into a draughty room.
> Then the vocal summits of the class
> with one boy at least in their midst
> dumb for an hour, mouthing air,
> the song-words flitting through his head,
> his eyes never leaving the inspector.

Here, the Sweeney 'control of form' (in Éilís Ní Dhuibhne's (1997) phrase) and his choice of word and image combine to convey an atmosphere which is chilling and sinister, a totally serious variation on moods which in other Sweeney poems become the embodiment of deep black 'absurd' comedy.

It is, however, on 'the Atlantic, starting, as it did at the bottom of the hill and visible from my bedroom window' that Sweeney in his 1993 article pins the label of 'biggest influence'. In a poem such as 'The House' the environmental landscape assumes a presence so strong that, whether we are thinking of the twelve-bedroomed house at its centre or of the ocean 'downhill half a mile', it takes on its own physicality of setting, never acting as a merely decorative backdrop. 'And I did grow up there' asserts the concluding line of 'The House', in the same sort of half-playful, half-wistful tone which, as we have already noted, is to be found in the closing line of 'A Boy' and is to be seen also in a poem such as 'Home', with its twelve-line bittersweet encapsulation of the sights and sounds of a terrain where 'high on a wooden beam a boy sits, a stopwatch in his hands'.

It is, incidentally, worth observing that the poem 'The House' first appeared in 1997 in one of Sweeney's adult collections, *The Bridal Suite*, before being included in *Up on the Roof*, the 'new and selected' (children's) poems in 2001. Clearly, this deliberate act of dual placing is the logical development of the point of view expressed by Sweeney in his 1993 article, to the effect that in his listing of the influences behind his poetry he makes 'no distinction' between his 'writing for adults and writing for children'. In *Writing Poetry and Getting Published*, a 'Teach Yourself' manual, which Sweeney co-wrote with John Hartley Williams (1997), the chapter entitled 'Writing for Children' summarises its central tenet as follows: '…in the act of writing poems for children you have to see through the eyes of a child while controlling these images and perceptions with your adult mind.' The chapter goes on to quote, with approval, PL Travers: 'If we're completely honest, not sentimental or nostalgic, we have no idea where childhood ends and maturity begins. It is one unending thread, not a life chopped up into sections out of touch with one another.' It is precisely the absence of nostalgia and sentimentality – in the terms Travers means here – which distinguishes Sweeney's poems of boyhood from so much in a similar genre. The adult mind's 'control' is permanently in evidence, as is the notion of 'one unending thread'. The 'boy' persona of many of these poems is, certainly, firmly fixed in that house, that yard, that beach, that ocean: but, as the numerous motifs of travel, escape and a world beyond make clear – 'And out there is *Iceland*' – the notion of continuity is implicit throughout.

Reference has already been made to how the 'chilling and sinister' dimension of some of Sweeney's poems becomes elsewhere in his work the departure lounge for flights into the domain of black 'absurd' humour. Depending on how far one wants to go to establish a literary ancestry for this strain in Sweeney, it is possible to think, among others, of Carroll, Lear, Belloc, Kafka, Beckett and Dahl, even Tom Lehrer. There are valid and potentially illuminating parallels in all of these and Kafka in particular is given some significance in the 'Writing for Children' chapter in *Writing*

Poetry and Getting Published. But the real key to Sweeney's 'blackness' and 'absurdity' perhaps lies in another reference in that chapter, to Elizabeth Bishop's phrase 'the surrealism of everyday life' (a phrase which also surfaces in the blurb to *The Bridal Suite* to describe Sweeney's preoccupations). Sweeney's emphasis on 'everyday life' as the background to even his most extravagant flights of fancy is what gives poems such as 'Johnjoe's Snowman' ('What he didn't tell/was that inside the snowman/he'd stuffed the cat'), 'Into the Mixer', 'Mr Bluejack' and the five poems in 'The Bad Girl Haiku' sequence their idiosyncratic frisson. In those poems such as 'Fishbones Dreaming', 'Cows on the Beach' and 'The Flying Spring Onion', where 'everyday life' serves as background for less macabre imaginings, the 'surrealism' often takes the form of diverting forays into the realm of nonsense – though this is a realm where, as in the mode of classic nonsense writing, nonsense has its own rules and logic amidst the anarchy and its own concerns with the playful possibilities of language. 'If you want to play the game of nonsense,' wrote Nancy Willard, 'the best way to start is by playing with words.' Sweeney's verbal frolics, which can range from the homophonic ambiguities of 'The Silent Knight' to the neologisms of 'After Dinner' ('a language for bored boys'), are one of his most engaging assets. ('And what children's poetry has in abundance,' says Sweeney in his introduction to *The New Faber Book of Children's Verse*, 'is a playfulness and inventiveness … all of these being qualities I like in poetry.')

The title poem of Sweeney's second collection – *Fatso in the Red Suit* – provides a convenient bridge for moving from his poetry to his prose. The length and detail (implicit and explicit) of this poem make it, in effect, a verse novella, one which focuses yet again on a boy, his growth and his developing insight into the ways of the adult world. Structured as a sequence of six episodes, the narrative seems initially to centre on the painful contrast between childhood innocence and adult knowingness, but the psychological complexities within the poem and its shifts, both stylistic and thematic, between child and adult viewpoint and between real and illusionary worlds are such that the reader's responses have to be constantly reconsidered.

Exactly the same comment may be made about Sweeney's first prose work for children, *The Chinese Dressing-Gown*, perhaps best described as a fable which pits childhood fascination with life's mysteries against dour adult scepticism – 'Really, Boo, it's time you put a stop to these imaginings,' says the child heroine's mother at one point – and in the process celebrates the curiosity of the young and their determination to gratify it. While the immediate setting of the story is clearly not Ireland, the country holds a central narrative significance as the birthplace of Boo's father, the father who appears both as the adult he is and as the ghost of the boy he was. In moving between these related, but differing, presences, Boo is intriguingly afforded the same insights as the reader of Sweeney's 'boyhood' poems – an understanding of the power of memory to transform our sense of time and place – but the insights in the novel are more painful in their acquisition.

The insights and understandings to be gleaned from Sweeney's second children's novel, *The Snow Vulture*, come in the form of even more searing experiences. Here, the authorial exploration of the young male psyche presents itself, in a narrative which concentrates on the rivalries of eleven-year-old identical twin brothers, as a dissection of obsession and of the potentially demonic nature of power. In literal terms, the opposed natures of Clive and Carl are memorably reflected in their opposed choice of subject for their snow sculptures, constructions so vividly realised that they possess a reality quite frightening in its solidity. In symbolic terms, they are dramatically counterpointed through a series of conflicting responses: the imaginative *versus* the rational, the natural *versus* the unnatural, the sane *versus* the mad. As in *Fatso and the Red Suit* and *The Chinese Dressing-Gown*, the foreground events are played out against a background of parent–child relationships which, if not overtly sinister, are nevertheless subtly disturbing. The solace which adult experience finds in boyhood memory elsewhere in Sweeney's work is not in evidence here, though the 'happy' resolution of the brothers' antagonism offers some measure of comfort.

In Sweeney's most recent novel, *Fox*, we return, however, to more positive notions of this intergenerational solace. Described on its cover as (a story of) 'A man, a boy and a … fox', this novel poignantly traces the quest of a young boy, adrift in a new school in a new city, for friendship. In a series of narrative circumstances he finds this in the companionship of an elderly homeless man and his pet fox. Their moments of shared joy and happiness become, for the boy, the beginning of his first journey into adult under-standing; for the man, who has spent much of his life travelling the world, they become the prelude to his departure on the journey which will be his last. The simple uncluttered style, the delicate balancing of child and adult perspectives and the sharply focused picture of inner city decay and dereliction all contribute to making *Fox* Sweeney's most powerful children's novel to date. At its heart is a boy's search for home, a motif which, as this essay has attempted to demonstrate, is a theme played with many modulations throughout his work and given expression in his various boyhood resurrections, whether his own or those of his fictional creations.

References

Ní Dhuibhne, Éilís (1997) 'Cruncher, Fatso and Skyscraper Ted: Contemporary Irish Poetry for Children' *The Lion and the Unicorn* 21(3)

Sweeney, Matthew (1993) 'Branching Out' *Children's Books in Ireland* 8

Sweeney, Matthew (2001) Introduction to *The New Faber Book of Children's Verse* London: Faber & Faber

Sweeney, Matthew and John Hartley Williams (1997) *Writing Poetry and Getting Published* London: Hodder 'Teach Yourself' Books

Willard, Nancy (1989) 'A Lively Last Word on Nonsense' in Celia Catlett Anderson and Marilyn Fain Apseloff (eds) *Nonsense Literature for Children* Hamden, CT: Library Professional Publications

Kate Thompson

By Robert Dunbar

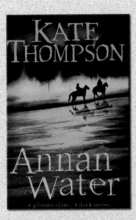

Titles by Kate Thompson

The Fourth Horseman (2006) The Bodley Head

The New Policeman (2005) The Bodley Head

Annan Water (2004) The Bodley Head

Origins (2003) The Bodley Head

The Alchemist's Apprentice (2002) The Bodley Head

The Beguilers (2001) The Bodley Head

Only Human (2001) The Bodley Head

The Missing Link (2000) The Bodley Head

Wild Blood (1999) The Bodley Head

Midnight's Choice (1998) The Bodley Head

Switchers (1997) The Bodley Head

Kate Thompson

By Robert Dunbar

> For a long time Bernard stood silently, observing the red-gold hairs. Then he looked up into Sandy's eyes again. 'Do you really wish you hadn't been born?' he said. Sandy held his gaze. She thought for a moment, then said, 'No. What I wish is that I'd been born human. Only human. That's all.'
>
> – Kate Thompson, from *Only Human*

The eleven novels that Kate Thompson has so far written for young readers are notable for the range and scope of their narratives. The plots of her Switchers trilogy – *Switchers*, *Midnight's Choice* and *Wild Blood* – are played out within a framework that, at both national and international level, encompasses climatic crisis and eco-politics. Genetic engineering and its complex morality serve as a backdrop for The Missing Link trilogy – *The Missing Link*, *Only Human* and *Origins* – and for *The Fourth Horseman*, each of them also informed by visions of impending societal disintegration: when we first meet the young narrator of the first of them he is reading a book called *Catastrophe Theory*. In *The Beguilers*, a richly imagined landscape, complete with its equally richly imagined flora and fauna, provides the setting for the allegorical story of its young heroine's quest for independence away from the confining conservatism of her immediate society. *The Alchemist's Apprentice* colourfully employs the genre of historical fiction to highlight a young boy's growing perception of the distinction between surface and substance. *Annan Water* effortlessly merges the words of a traditional folksong into a dark, contemporary story of adolescent romance. Equally effortlessly, *The New Policeman* merges contemporary family life in the west of Ireland and ancient Irish legend. It is by way of the intriguing variety of plot, characterisation and setting within these novels that we are guided to the equally intriguing variations that Thompson plays on what is clearly the dominant theme in her work: a concern with the meaning of the word 'human' and with the rights and responsibilities that are attached to it.

It might initially seem strange that Thompson should have first chosen to explore this concern in a trilogy where, as its Switchers title implies, the focus is on shape-changing, on moving between human and non-human identity. But, as Marina Warner's *Fantastic Metamorphoses, Other Worlds* (significantly subtitled *Ways of Telling the Self*) reminds us, in the context of discussing some of the shape-changers in Ovid's *Metamorphoses*, 'the shape into which they shift more fully expresses them and perfects them than their first form'. This is a comment that could be fairly made not merely on Thompson's central 'switchers', Tess and Kevin, but also on their numerous ancestors in the protean world of Irish myth and legend, the terrain that bequeaths a distinct literary and thematic heritage to the Thompson novels.

'You can't just end up as a polar bear or a walrus. You're human, Kevin, you have to be human!' says Tess in *Switchers*, though at this early stage in their friendship she is not quite able to articulate her understanding in greater detail. By the time of *Midnight's Choice*, as she attempts to intercede between vampire and phoenix, she is 'desperate for the full use of the human mind to work out what was going on'. When we come to *Wild Blood* she has grown sufficiently to understand – and accept – that 'along with her human form [come] all its attendant miseries', though it is in Kevin's words that the trilogy's final understanding is expressed: 'What matters is that being a Switcher taught me ... taught you as well, Tess ... how to adapt. How to change to meet whatever situation arises, even though we might look to some form outside.' The young people have flirted (often enjoyably, sometimes dangerously) with some of what Warner calls 'the possible permutations of personal identity' – and have finally embraced their own.

In *Frankenstein's Footsteps: Science, Genetics and Popular Culture*, Jon Turney points out how, as regards contemporary developments in the biological sciences, 'the power of the new experimental biology to tap feelings of deep ambivalence is now very familiar'. Exploration of this 'deep ambivalence' lies at the heart of Thompson's excursions, in The Missing Link trilogy into what Turney summarises as the theme of the Frankenstein myth, 'the getting and using of knowledge and the power that knowledge may confer'. As in the Switchers trilogy, the essential focus is on shift and change. But here the setting is the scientific laboratory and the moral dilemmas are those that derive from aspirations to manipulate and control.

At the outset of *The Missing Link* these adult urges are perceived through the eyes of Christie, a thirteen-year-old, presented as someone willing 'to accept without understanding that there [are] more things in the world than he had ever dreamt of'. As events develop, however, this acceptance is to shift from mere acquiescence to a much more informed clarification, which comes to him, in *Only Human*, via his meeting with the abbot of a Tibetan monastery. It is this mentor figure (a recurring type in Thompson's fiction) who persuades the boy to see the phrase 'only human' as an aid to liberation rather than imprisonment. 'Think,' says the abbot, 'what it might mean for humanity if being only human were not taken as an excuse for weakness and self-indulgence, but as the challenge it ought to be.'

In literary and structural terms, the novels of The Missing Link trilogy are Thompson's least successful books: the 'journey' motif in each of them is too protracted, there are too many diversions (of various sorts) along the way. But in their ability – particularly in their portrayal of Sandy and her anguished relationship with her scientist father – to impel us to reflect on our brave new biotechnological world and such people as may be in it, they are extremely stimulating. It is, however, in a later novel, *The Fourth Horseman*, that Thompson's interest in biotechnological themes (and in the teasing out of another father–daughter relationship) is given its most accomplished treatment. Its combination of individual, national and global concerns acts as a powerful framework for what becomes a narrative characterised by tension and suspense, as we follow fifteen-year-old Laurie McAllister's account of the complications ensuing for herself, her mother and her brother when her virologist father is determined to pursue 'monumental discoveries' in the realm of 'cutting-edge genetic engineering'. This research – involving experimentation on squirrels – has its own fascinatingly esoteric dimension and is treated in a much more accessible manner than a similar theme, involving cats and dogs, in *Origins*. But its real significance in the novel has more to do with the ethical issues that it raises: might it eventually amount to what one of Laurie's friends describes as 'a recipe for genocide'?

Thompson's concern to link the work of the individual in his laboratory with what is going on in the wider contemporary world evinces a strong awareness of the potential of social and political developments – 'the perilous state the world was in' – to be the harbingers of eventual destruction. It is in pursuit of this concern that she introduces into the realistic domains of her novel the apocalyptic figures of the four horsemen of the New Testament's The Revelation of St John the Divine, who come to stand, in Laurie's own words, 'like a backdrop to the political situation', a phrase which, in its context, may fairly be taken to refer to 'politics' in both its domestic and governmental senses. Laurie and her father's various sightings of these sinister and emblematic apparitions provide some of the novel's most striking metaphors for glimpses of a Yeatsian world where things are threatening to fall apart, where the moral centre is being undermined by talk of terrorism and war. If at times all of this might seem to result in a novel over-rich in its literal and symbolic weighting, the flaw is minimised by the strength of the portrayal of its narrator, Laurie, who demonstrates her 'human' aspect in an engaging (and largely plausible) adolescent combination of apparent precocity and certain self-delusion.

The global understandings of Laurie about 'the perilous state the world was in' move, in Thompson's *The New Policeman*, from macrocosmic to microcosmic level, as we embark on a west of Ireland novel which starts with reminders of how 'street gangs' are 'engaging in all kinds of thuggery and muggery' in Galway City. But while such intimations of social upheaval and details hinting at environmental maltreatment are to be alluded to occasionally in the course of the narrative its principal focus becomes much more domestic, as we meet JJ, its fifteen-year-old hero confronting gossipy rumours about alleged secrets and cover-ups in his family history. The structural and thematic crossover from JJ's everyday Kinvara world to the world of Irish myth and legend – a domain first drawn on by Thompson in her Switchers trilogy – is handled here with an ease and credibility in which ingenuity, humour and poignancy are skilfully blended. The principal link is supplied by JJ's awareness of how, in his present day Ireland, there never seems to be enough time for him – or for anyone else, but especially his mother – to accommodate the numerous demands competing for their attention. His subsequent determination to amend this state of affairs is to lead eventually to Tír na nÓg, in which and from which perspectives of time are viewed very differently. These perceptions are voiced by a diverting range of whimsical characters from the 'stories and superstitions' of ancient Ireland.

Thompson's tone in all of this is reminiscent of that of James Stephens in his *Irish Fairy Tales*, not least in her laconic idiom and wittily etched characterisation. ('He's so underrated,' Thompson has said of Stephens in an interview given to Eileen Battersby in early 2006.) The parallel with Stephens is at its most obvious in the roles (or role) given, in the 'real' world and in the fairy world, to the tutelary spirit of Aengus – 'the wild Irishman, with his fiddle and his charm and his little bit of magic', as one of his shape-changing fellow inhabitants of a past Ireland describes him. That 'little bit of magic' – and the need to preserve it in the face of forces which have threatened and, *mutatis mutandis*, continue to threaten a country in whose 'far-distant history people moved freely between the two worlds' – is symbolised throughout Thompson's narrative by the restorative and life-enhancing qualities ascribed to music, seen by Larry, our new policeman, as 'linking his past to his present'. (Shades of Stephens again, when in his story 'The Boyhood of Fionn' the young hero and his friends are debating as to what is the finest music in the world: 'The music of what happens,' proposes Fionn, 'that is the finest music in the world.') The attribution of this central symbolic role to the power of music endows the novel with a pervasive warmth and richness, complemented by the inclusion within the text of a selection of Irish melodies: the precise placing of these affords various examples of mischievous and ironic juxtaposition. Music, in essence, has a unifying, harmonising and humanising effect on the events and characters of the novel, a role which accentuates communal values and virtues. In terms of its overall excellence, *The New Policeman* is Thompson's finest achievement, a worthy winner of its many awards; it may well, as Celia Keenan (2005) has argued, 'become a classic'.

Music, in the form of the words and melody of a haunting folksong, is central also to the thematic and structural development of Thompson's *Annan Water*, a novel which makes a powerful and original contribution to the hackneyed genre of turbulent teenage romance. Its most distinguishing feature is its magical blend of person and place. An ancient ballad's 'dark expanse of water' and the tragedy buried beneath it come strongly into focus as we follow teenagers Michael and Annie in their attempt to share and exorcise their own past traumas. The tortured histories and current circumstances of both their families, the isolated Scottish setting and the hardships of economic survival in the competitive world of horse-trading and show-jumping combine to create a sequence of barriers to easy resolution, but Thompson's sympathy with the need of the young to articulate and fulfil their dreams is never in question. 'If there is a common thread to my books,' Thompson has said in an interview with Julia Eccleshare (2005), 'it is that each involves an individual journey. The individual must stay true to themselves.' In *Annan Water* the tracing of the two individual journeys at its centre moves from a dramatic first encounter to a series of almost unbearable developments in the young couple's seemingly inexorable progress towards destruction, developments played out against a storm of 'some awful, flapping, apocalyptic enormity, born of the wild wind'.

Almost from the moment of that first encounter the relationship bristles with sexual tension and yearning: 'She wasn't only in his mind at school the following day. His whole skin was full of her. She inhabited his flesh. He felt her rings and studs in his face, her scars on his forearms, the lightness and grace of her feminine limbs. Her expressions, her gestures emanated from him.' But, just as powerful as these elemental enormities and adolescent passions, there is the additional narrative to be found originally in the ballad of the book's title: once sung by Michael's grandmother, it now becomes the novel's leitmotif. Rather as Michael feels at one moment that he is being 'summoned' by the 'deep song' of the Annan, the reader is impelled by Thompson's mesmeric prose to enter a state of total surrender to a narrative that never loses its hold. The style and structure, though spare and short in the succession of short chapters, still manages to allow room for interweaving fictions which, at times, are heartbreaking in their poignancy.

The necessity to acknowledge the 'challenge' implicit in being 'only human', as suggested by the abbot to Christie in *Only Human* and which we see once again as a key theme in *Annan Water*, is accepted at that moment in Thompson's *The Beguilers* when Rilka, its young heroine, has her first close-up encounter with one of the creatures who give the novel its title. 'Somehow,' she reflects, 'I learned that being human was painful; a thing to be pitied.' And later, when she has determined that her 'Great Intention' will be to catch one, even if such a decision breaks all her society's traditions, she asks rhetorically, 'After all, what's the point of being human and having choices in life if everyone just ends up behaving like cattle?'

Her journey through the 'were-woods' and into the cloud mountains culminates in her discovery that responsibility for the creation of 'the beguilers' resides within her own culture, a culture that has employed its 'chuffies' to absorb 'all its sorrow and anger and upset' and has now to pay the price as the chuffies' souls return, in beguiler form, to claim their payment. (Pythagorean notions of the transmigration of souls join forces here with notions of bodily transformation.) The question posed in *Wild Blood* by Lizzie, the mentor figure of the Switchers books, comes to mind: 'Does we believe what we sees ... or does we see what we believe?' Being human may, indeed, be 'painful, a thing to be pitied', but our growth towards maturity starts when these become our points of departure as distinct from a signal for submission.

On one level an engrossing story of a young woman who dares disturb her universe, *The Beguilers* additionally takes its readers into philosophical and political domains where the manner in which we order our society and the individual's role within it are subjected to invigorating scrutiny.

As virtually every commentator on Thompson's *The Alchemist's Apprentice* has, quite rightly, pointed out, its central concern is encapsulated in a question that Jonathan Barnstable, the alchemist, puts to fourteen-year-old Jack at an early stage in his apprenticeship: 'Which matters more? Gold in the hand or gold in the spirit?' It seems totally appropriate that Thompson, a writer so interested in her earlier work in matters of transformation and mutation, should eventually turn her attention to alchemy, a subject which, wherever its metaphorical associations may take us, starts, quite literally, with change. When we meet Jack in the book's opening chapter he is, we are told, too busy in his work in the farrier's forge 'to sit around and reflect upon the series of misfortunes that constituted his existence or to contemplate what possible future a boy like himself might expect'. But change sets in almost immediately in his decision to leave the forge and in his embarking on his travels into the multipatterned if often deceptively attractive world of alchemy. From the moment when, in Barnstable's workshop, Jack first sees the portraits of the Red King and the White Queen (emblematic of the red sulphur and white lead conjoined in the alchemic process) and of Hermes, 'the divine child ... the desired end of all our efforts', he is haunted by these iconographic representations of the magical pursuit whose arcane mysteries he hopes to penetrate. With, however, further changes in his circumstances and, especially, in his growing material prosperity, come new insights into the consequences of misdirected desire. Just as the Tibetan monks had pointed out to Christie in *Only Human* how 'desire is the cause of all suffering', the realisation comes eventually to Jack that 'the only things that were to blame for his disappointment were his own desires and expectations'. By the time we leave Jack on the book's final page, tossing his precious athanor into the river that will soon carry it 'towards the hungry streets of London town', he has travelled through his 'long, painful darkness' to arrive at a stage of dazzling enlightenment. Like Kevin at the end of *Switchers*, he has learned 'to find for himself the invisible path which lies between what is and what isn't'.

In delineating the destinies of the young protagonists of these eleven novels, Thompson has shown remarkable insight into the dreams and disenchantments of young humanity and its dawning perception that growth, in its various manifestations, can develop only by way of some delicate act of balance between the two. There are many such epiphanic realisations within her work, though few with the potency of the moment when, after his sojourn in the wider world, Jack is reunited with his 'master', Barnstable. 'Tell me about delusion,' the alchemist demands; the balancing process begins. We, the readers, realise here (as we have realised elsewhere in these novels) that the art of the alchemist and the art of the storyteller, both endowed with creative power and imaginative energy, have much in common: the necessary metamorphosis that we recognise in both of their pursuits embodies, in Warner's phrase, 'the condition of writing itself'. Regularly in Thompson's work, and especially in her most accomplished novels such as *The Beguilers*, *The Alchemist's Apprentice*, *Annan Water* and *The New Policeman*, the quality of that writing is such that it can be seen to parallel the numerous 'changing moods' that Rilka diagnoses in the extraordinary repertoire of the nightangel's song in *The Beguilers*, moods that range from 'plaintive sobbing to sparkling chickering to melodic passages that stun … with their simple beauty'. These are the tunes of which the condition of being human is composed.

References

Battersby, Eileen (2006) 'Poised in a Land between Worlds' *The Irish Times* January 21

Eccleshare, Julia (2005) 'The Music of Time' *Inis* 14

Keenan, Celia (2005) Review of *The New Policeman*, *Inis* 12

Turney, Jon (1998) *Frankenstein's Footsteps: Science, Genetics and Popular Culture* New Haven and London: Yale University Press

Warner, Marina (2002) *Fantastic Metamorphoses, Other Worlds* Oxford: Oxford University Press

Martin Waddell

By Lucy O'Dea

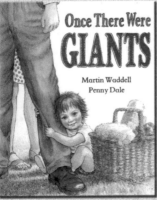

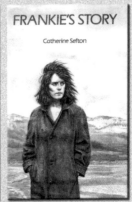

Selected titles by Martin Waddell

Picturebooks
Room for a Little One, with Jason Cockcroft (2005) Orchard
A Kitten Called Moonlight,
with Christian Birmingham (2001) Candlewick
John Joe and the Big Hen, with Paul Howard (1995) Walker
The Big Big Sea, with Jennifer Eachus (1994) Walker
Owl Babies, with Patrick Benson (1992) Walker
The Pig in the Pond, with Jill Barton (1992) Walker
Farmer Duck, with Helen Oxenbury (1991) Walker
Grandma's Bill, with Jane Johnson (1990) Macdonald
Once There Were Giants, with Penny Dale (1989) Walker
The Park in the Dark, with Barbara Firth (1989) Walker
Can't You Sleep, Little Bear? with Barbara Firth (1988) Walker

Novels
(all except *Tango's Baby* originally published
under the name Catherine Sefton)
Tango's Baby (1996) Walker
The Beat of the Drum (1988) Hamish Hamilton
(republished 2001 by Walker)
Frankie's Story (1988) Hamish Hamilton (republished 2001 by Walker)
Starry Night (1986) Hamish Hamilton (republished 2001 by Walker)
Island of the Strangers (1983) Hamish Hamilton
Emer's Ghost (1981) Hamish Hamilton

Story collection
The Orchard Book of Ghostly Stories, with Sophy Williams (2000) Orchard

Martin Waddell

By Lucy O'Dea

Martin Waddell's work encompasses challenging and thought-provoking novels for older readers and fun-filled picturebooks for young children, short stories, novels for newly independent readers and a series of books about Napper McCann and his football career.

One of the most notable features of Waddell's diverse and wide-ranging body of work is an acute awareness of and respect for the reader. This is evident not only in what he chooses to write about but also in the way he treats his themes and subjects at different levels. Many of his picturebooks look at children confronting fear and conquering it in the warm shelter of adult support, whereas the consequences of the absence of adult support are seen in some of his novels for older readers. At all age levels he deals with the everyday concerns and emotions of children but he is not afraid to ask the reader to consider big questions and tackle serious matters.

In *Can't You Sleep, Little Bear?*, the first and probably best known of the five Little Bear stories, Waddell demonstrates to the reader that fear is normal and understandable. Little Bear cannot sleep because of his fear of the dark so Big Bear tries to help by bringing him ever bigger lanterns. The patience with which Big Bear overcomes his exasperation each time he has to put down his book and attend to Little Bear is revealed with gentle humour. Bracketed asides indicate how little reading he manages to achieve between interruptions: '…putting down his Big Bear book (which was just getting to the interesting part)' or '(with just four pages to go to the interesting bit)'. Little Bear's need for company and adult reassurance is also defined in the spare text: 'Little Bear tried and tried to go to sleep but he couldn't', which leaves room for the illustrations to show the humorous antics of Little Bear 'trying' to go asleep. Nothing works until finally Big Bear takes him outside into the night and helps him to confront his fear. Through the character of Big Bear, who accepts without question each time Little Bear points out a new source of darkness, Waddell shows that the way to deal with fear is to face up to it, but he places a caring and guiding adult in the picture to reassure the reader that it doesn't have to be faced alone. In this story, as in the following Little Bear book, *Let's Go Home Little Bear*, the problem is only solved and the fear dispelled when he is safe in the arms of Big Bear. This warm and reassuring presence of a guiding adult is maintained through all the Little Bear books in the character of Big Bear, while Little Bear gradually learns how to get by in the world around him, as he reaches towards independence. The exact nature of the relationship between Big Bear and Little Bear is never spelt out, so the stories can be fitted into the context of the reader's own experience.

Sleep Tight, Little Bear is the fifth and latest of the Little Bear stories. Echoes of the first title underline the sense of closure suggested in this title. Little Bear has taken his first steps alone in the wide world and is almost ready for his own bear cave. Helped and supported by Big Bear, he sets it up and moves in. In very few words Waddell captures the poignancy and resignation of such important moments: 'Big Bear plodded all the way back to the cave alone, without Little Bear.' Feeling rather small, however, and all alone in his Big Bear cave, Little Bear heads home so that Big Bear won't be lonely. With characteristically delicate text and gentle humour Waddell demonstrates the gradual and tentative nature of the journey towards independence.

Like the Little Bear books, *The Park in the Dark* and *Owl Babies* are two further examples of how Waddell deals with particular fears (fear of the dark and fear of abandonment), and more universal fears, which may linger on into adulthood – fear of the unknown and fear of the wide world outside and beyond immediate experience. Stylistically, he helps the young reader to cope with facing these fears. He draws the reader into the narrative with strong and engaging characterisation and repetitive text and encourages identification by using lots of dialogue. Although Waddell encourages engagement, he helps the reader, at the same time, to maintain a comfortable distance by using animal characters and by the gentle humour which demonstrates how unfounded a fear can sometimes be, while also acknowledging that fear is sometimes appropriate. The support for coping in *Owl Babies* and in *The Park in the Dark* comes not from a guiding adult but from the safety of numbers, as 'me and Loopy and Little Gee' venture out to the park together, while Sarah and Percy and Bill, the three little owls, wait anxiously but together for their mother's return. The three 'Owl Babies' cope with their mother's absence in different ways. Sarah, the eldest, tries to be strong and optimistic, Percy, the middle one following her lead, struggles to be brave. Only Bill, the smallest one, reveals his true state of anxiety in the repeated refrain 'I want my Mummy'. Once again, the reader is left to engage at a personal level, invited to speculate about the outcome and identify with the emotion. Mindful of his readers, Waddell provides reassurance in a satisfying outcome.

In some of his other books Waddell employs a more high-spirited kind of humour. *The Pig in the Pond* is a hilarious but deceptively simple story of Nelligan's pig, who gets hotter and hotter in the sunny farmyard. Unable to bear it any longer he finds the obvious but unprecedented solution of jumping into the duck pond. In this exuberantly told tale, Waddell once again challenges his young readers to consider important matters about the human condition. The repetition of 'She didn't go in because pigs don't swim' underlines the stifling effect of an overly conformist society. The shock expressed by the other animals as the word spreads of a pig in the pond and the rush to view the uncharacteristic spectacle demonstrate the difficulty of expressing individuality. Once again, however, a supporting adult in the shape of farmer Nelligan is on hand. Surprising all, he jumps in the pond too, showing the other animals and the reader that diversity is not only acceptable, but welcome.

Farmer Duck, also set on a farm, is quite different. Waddell concerns himself frequently with the effect that being born into a specific family and into a particular set of circumstances has on the lives of individuals. It is a preoccupation of his Northern trilogy and of his novels for older readers. Here, it is presented at an appropriate level for his younger readers and made clear from the opening line, 'There once was a duck who had the bad luck to live with a lazy old farmer.' The powerlessness of the duck to change his situation is also implied. The farmer oversees the work from afar, while the duck wearily but resignedly carries out all the chores. Once again, the support of others is the way ahead. Their simple but very powerful reason for helping is expressed in the most concise and direct language: 'The hens and the cow and the sheep got very upset. They loved the duck.' The farmer is dealt with by all the farmyard animals and (with echoes of Orwell's *Animal Farm*) faces the consequences of his actions. The resolution of the story and the future of all the animals is suggested in the natural and unforced language characteristic of Waddell, as 'they all set to work on their farm'.

Families of all kinds loom large in the work of Martin Waddell, whether writing under his own name or his alter ego of Catherine Sefton. Many of his best-loved picturebooks such as *John Joe and the Big Hen* show small children growing up amid the daily interactions of family life, while books like *The Big Big Sea*, *A Kitten Called Moonlight* and *My Great Grandpa* demonstrate very powerfully the close and loving relationship between caring adults and children. *Once There Were Giants*, *Grandma's Bill* and *Rosie's Babies* show the cycle of family life and remind children how they can cope at times of upheaval and crisis.

Room for a Little One, Waddell's treatment of the nativity story, also retains the traditional elements but offers a different perspective. Ox begins the night alone in his stable. With words of kindness he gradually fills it up with various animals. When the tired donkey and his weary travelling companions arrive they too are invited to share the warmth and companionship, since 'There's always room for a little one here'. Underpinning the message of Christmas, the animals look out for each other, suspend natural animosity and welcome Jesus to the warmth of their stable. With understated narrative and a gentle refrain, Waddell evokes a sense of peace and harmony and invites his readers to identify with the message.

The hard-hitting and often disturbing novels for older readers deal more specifically with the frailty and vulnerability of the human condition. Families in these stories are more likely to display some level of dysfunction. *Tango's Baby* tells of two mismatched teenagers, whose relationship is doomed to failure from the outset, despite their efforts to prove everyone wrong.

Brian Tangello and Crystal O'Leary are an unlikely couple. Brian is a simple but flawed character, not adept at thinking things through but capable of great love, demonstrated throughout, not only in his feelings for Crystal but also in his tenderness towards his granny. Crystal's family circumstances are also difficult and when her dad dies she comes upon Tango in a moment of need. They are held together for a time by that need and then by her pregnancy and the birth of their son. This is a complex and sophisticated narrative, in which the lives of many characters are inextricably interwoven. Events are narrated retrospectively by Chris, a friend of Tango, giving the reader a personalised view of the events of the story and resulting in a close engagement with the characters. Characterisation as with all of Waddell's books is very sure. Well-drawn and credible individuals make the reader care what happens, a very powerful strategy in this novel, as the reader knows from the outset that there is no happy ending. This is a device used on a number of occasions by Waddell. In this story it creates a haunting sense of inevitability underlined by the final words – '"I know Tango was the one who got hammered," I said. "He was always going to," Madonna said' – and brings an element of despondency to the narrative, which Waddell balances by the warmth of characterisation and a degree of humour. At the same time it creates a tension and drives the story forward, as the reader anxiously anticipates the dénouement with a heightened awareness of the chain of events that lead to the conclusion.

Waddell often employs the point of view of his young protagonists to recruit the reader into the action and to heighten the atmosphere of a story. This can be seen in many of his ghost stories. The ghosts are generally benign and following an initial uneasiness engage the sympathy of the young, frequently female characters, to whom they appear. Many of these characters have undergone a traumatic experience in their own lives. Ellen in *Back House Ghost* has suffered the death of her father and a complete upheaval of her normal way of life. In *Emer's Ghost* the father is also dead and Emer, very conscious of the hardship of her mother's life, feels a deep sense of responsibility towards her. The ghosts in these stories are usually seeking help with unresolved issues, although in the case of Waddell's first ghost story, *The Ghost in the Blue Velvet Dress*, the ghost of the title comes not to seek but to offer help. Generally there is a fitting resolution and a satisfying closure for the reader at the end of the narrative. One of the key elements in these stories is the way the past impinges on the present and the effect this has on the daily lives of the characters. *The Ghost Girl* is probably the most political of the ghost stories. It places the Irish situation in a historical context and concludes, 'If they are the victims of Irish History, then so are we … but they are dead, and we still have a chance to choose. We can try to find another way.'

Although Waddell returns in the more recent collection, *The Orchard Book of Ghostly Stories*, to the subject of ghosts, this very atmospheric book is somewhat different. The eight ghost stories here are deliberately written to read as old traditional tales. They have a pattern and a cadence like stories that have been handed down orally and retold over generations. In fact they are all original, apart from 'Little Bridget', a story based on Allingham's poem 'The Fairies'. As in all of his stories, a sense of place is important and with striking language he conjures up images of a misty Irish countryside. Although quite different in many ways from his previous writing, it bears all the hallmarks of a Waddell/Sefton creation – finely crafted and carefully honed language with no spare words, gripping narrative which engages and involves the reader in the events of the story, satisfying resolutions and a respectful awareness of his audience.

A ghostly tale forms the background for *Island of the Strangers* and there is a real sense of a past interwoven into current happenings. The story, constructed around the visit of a group of city children to a small village, presents a view of a society divided by fear and prejudice, which is continuously reinforced by gossip and rumour. Adults and children alike display an intolerance of difference where anything outside their immediate experience is seen as suspicious and threatening. People are judged by appearance and entrenched opinions are delivered as fact. There is a sense of tribalism among the young people and a conviction that it is not possible to remain neutral: 'If you're not with us you're against us.' Nora, the main character, has no desire to be part of the conflict. Neither does Crystal, her counterpart in the city group, but there is an awful inevitability once again in the way their interactions with the group draw them further and further in.

Fear, prejudice and the inevitability of being caught up in a situation are explored in some detail in the three books that deal specifically with the Northern Ireland conflict. There is an overt and conscious ideology at work here as Waddell strives to present a balanced view of both sides of the conflict. One of the most disturbing aspects of the stories is the way in which ideologies are absorbed by young people, evident in the way in which the lives of the characters are shaped by the places in which they live and the circumstances of their lives. Through his vivid and detailed characterisation and a wide range of colourful supporting characters, Waddell demonstrates how prejudice is handed down from generation to generation and inculcated from an early age. Looking at events from three different perspectives he highlights the fundamental sameness of people, demonstrates how fear and ignorance are at the heart of much conflict and advocates the need for acceptance on all sides.

Although *Starry Night* does not focus specifically on the 'Troubles', they inform characterisation and provide a significant backdrop to the story, which has references to army patrols, 'United Ireland' and 'the blast hole at Cone Cross'. Waddell uses supporting characters to expose Kathleen to an alternative way of thinking, in particular her friend Ann from Belfast and her sister-in-law Carmel who brings an outsider's perspective. At the end of the story she is moved to question her own values: '…but where had I got my dreams from? Maybe the dreams were just a trap.'

Frankie's Story, a dark and complex tale of family drama and domestic upheaval, presents a more closely focused view of the Troubles. In this case, the Catholic teenager Frankie is directly and personally affected by the conflict and by the end of the story has left Northern Ireland and is living in England. This book closes with Frankie's words, 'Nobody's going to lay down what I should or shouldn't think, or should or shouldn't be.' Ironically, it is only from the distance of another country that she is free to hope and plan a future.

Brian Hanna's story in *The Beat of the Drum* is different. His disability allows him to remain outside of the immediacy of the conflict. It is also a device by which Waddell has invested in him a more distanced perspective of his own Protestant community. It is left to supporting characters – his uncle, his friends and their families – to present the bigoted positions, which eventually lead to tragedy. Ultimately, though, for Brian, the future remains in Belfast and he concludes by saying, 'I am responsible. That's why I am staying here.'

In these, as in all of his books, Waddell calls upon his reader to think and to question. First-person narratives, which place his characters right at the heart of a conflict situation, contribute to this. Honest and truthful, he presents the grey areas of life and offers no false hope. Actions in these stories have consequences. Yet here, as in all of his work, Waddell is mindful of his readers, never closing the door completely on deliverance. In his work for younger children a positive resolution is very present in the narrative. It is less obvious in the books for older readers and requires some effort to find. In the absence of cosy endings the reader is encouraged to speculate on the outcome, as characters strive to come to terms with their situations and find a way to cope with their reality.

Waddell's wide range of writing has been well recognised in the many awards and nominations he has received during the course of his writing career. From the minimal but highly expressive and carefully crafted text in his picturebooks, in which he leaves room for the added dimension of the illustrator, to the complex but equally crafted stories for older readers, he continues to entertain and amuse, engaging and challenging readers of all ages. He deals with the ordinary and complex lives of individuals and their concerns and shows that there are many different ways of seeing and many ways for human beings to live together.

In 2004, Martin Waddell was awarded IBBY's Hans Christian Andersen award for a lifetime's contribution to children's literature.

Gerard Whelan

By Carole Redford

Titles by Gerard Whelan

Novels
War Children (2002) O'Brien
Out of Nowhere (1999) O'Brien
A Winter of Spies (1998) O'Brien
Dream Invader (1997) O'Brien
The Guns of Easter (1996) O'Brien

Short stories
'Immigrants' (2002) in Polly Nolan (ed) *Giants of the Sun* Macmillan
'Thesaurus' (2001) in Robert Dunbar (ed) *Skimming* O'Brien
'Jailbirds of a Feather' (1998)
in Gerard Whelan (ed) *Big Pictures* Lucan Educate Together School

Gerard Whelan

By Carole Redford

Both the opening sentence of Gerard Whelan's novel *Out of Nowhere*, 'First there was nothing at all', and the title itself echo the first two verses of the Book of Genesis. But, unlike God, Whelan does not look down on the world he has made and pronounce it good. Whelan doesn't mean it to be so. For his universe, unlike that of the Divine, does not emerge from a void, but from a contemporary Ireland of which Whelan is critical. His fiction, while often containing scathing attacks on modern society, recognises too the wonderful idiocy that runs through it. The notion that underpins *Out of Nowhere* that 'it's a funny old world', coupled with less philosophical and more censorious observations, pervades his writing. They are wonderfully fused in his 'horror' novel *Dream Invader*; and they combine with the depiction of the savagery of conflict in his historical fiction, *The Guns of Easter*, its sequel *A Winter of Spies*, and *War Children*.

At the centre of Whelan's writing is a concern for, and fascination with, the destruction of childhood innocence by forces, often violent forces, outside the control of the young. His child protagonists are often the unwitting victims of corrupt adult behaviour. This is evident in his war fiction, in which children are confronted with traumatic situations due to the antagonism of an adult world rent asunder by factional fighting. It is no accident that the historical background to his work deals with the trauma surrounding the emergence of an autonomous Ireland, and that this is mirrored in the portrayal of the equally harrowing emergence into independence of Whelan's young protagonists.

The propulsion of children into the adult world of experience is a dominant theme in his latest work to date, *War Children,* a collection of short stories set at the time of the War of Independence. It is arguably the most impressive book of Irish short stories for the young since the publication of Ré Ó Laighléis's critically acclaimed taut and uncompromising *Ecstasy and Other Stories* (Poolbeg 1992). In 'Mulligan's Drop', possibly the finest story in the book, the young protagonist, Statia, who longs to be treated as mature, is caught up in an ambush at, significantly, a bridge, for the trauma of the episode projects her out of her childhood innocence into the horror of the adult world. Whelan tells us that 'she wasn't a child now; in her blank terror she was *hardly* even human', and a paragraph later he uses the image of waking up to suggest a new beginning (reminiscent of Stephen's experience in the opening scene of *Out of Nowhere*): 'When she woke up she lay looking at the sky, wondering where and who and what she was.' While the repetition of the word 'and' encapsulates the girl's fear and confusion, it is through the characteristically Whelanesque device of intermingling the potentially comic, even burlesque, with the horrific (as, for instance, in the almost Laurel and Hardy moment in *The Guns of Easter* when the corpulent dead body of Uncle Charlie lands on top of little Jimmy Conway) that the reader is confronted by the grotesque nature of Statia's trauma: 'The dead man lay grinning at Statia, like someone who'd been frozen in the act of playing "peep" with her. Peep! said the dead man's grin. I sees you there.' This image captures perfectly and graphically the moment when innocence is banished. Statia's youth and naïveté could at first conceive of nothing beyond the world of childhood, of play; she then becomes suddenly aware that she is staring into the face of death. The makebelieve fright of childhood inherent in the game of 'peep' is horrifically transformed into animal terror, as innocence is violated by experience.

The transforming event, as in so much of Whelan's fiction, is death, as Sarah realises in *A Winter of Spies*:

> Death was the main thing. They might all speak of freedom and honour, but what it seemed to come down to in the end was always death. She could feel Da's arm enclosing hers as she walked along saying the word to herself under her breath: 'Death.'

> She realised that death had never been real to her before. It had been a sort of idea.
> Now the word had a new and deeper sound when she said it. It was no longer so easy
> to say. Before this it had only been a word. Now it was a spray of bright red blood, foun-
> taining out of a man's neck, from a hole put there by someone she'd sat and talked with.

The realisation of the horror of death is what separates adults from the world of childhood. It is, then, no wonder that in *Out of Nowhere* we are told that those who remember life before their universe was transformed 'are all hopelessly mad'; the pain of remembering is such that one man 'says nothing at all – except sometimes he howls'. The first words the protagonist, Stephen, hears are 'You're awake, young man', suggesting the dawning of experience, the coming to full consciousness of the world he inhabits. To remain sane in the world of experience, it seems it is necessary to forget what has been. To realise one's loss, the implication is, is too much for the human psyche to bear.

Whelan's conviction about the corrupt nature of the adult world is intimately bound up with notions of masculinity. War is portrayed as a largely male construct, exemplified by the expression on Hugh Byrne's face in *A Winter of Spies,* which, we are told, 'had been wide and happy and it had taken the prospect of killing somebody to put it there'. This is contrasted with Lily Conway's 'war', which consisted of 'the fight to feed her children and keep her family whole and safe', a conflict undertaken also by her young adolescent son, Jimmy. For here, as elsewhere in his fiction, Whelan is never simplistic. Lily's husband joins the British army to prevent his family from starving, a position which combines his masculine lust for war with the female desire to nurture.

The notion of corruption and the divergence of the sexes reaches its height in Whelan's writing with the myth of the Pooshipaw, the eponymous dream invader. The very notion of an invader, as Whelan's historical fiction demonstrates, is one wrapped up with notions of force, intrusion and encroachment. Given this, and considering the date of publication – 1997 – *Dream Invader* is much more than a story of the powers of evil attempting the destruction of an innocent young child. It emerges from a society irate and traumatised by the scandals of child sexual abuse concerning revered figures of authority in the two previously unassailable institutions of the state, the family and the church. Each society formulates the monsters whose characteristics reflect the fears and the perceived evils that assail the population. As Birdie Murray explains, 'there is more than one Pooshipaw in the world .... Anybody with knowledge could make a Pooshipaw, and the kind of Pooshipaw they made would depend on the ingredients that they put into it – like a cake.'

It is no accident that the horrors little Simon experiences are perpetrated in bed, the area associated with the security, vulnerability and privacy of sleep, but also with sexual activity, a notion underlined by the bed being made in the image of a sports car, that well-known emblem of male sexual fantasy. As is the custom with paedophiles, the Pooshipaw purports to be the child's friend. The use and abuse of the word 'sausage' as a term of endearment captures brilliantly the duplicity of the monster. It is a masterly stroke by Whelan, encapsulating condescension but implying familiarity and affection, notions which are violated by the creature's subsequent behaviour. The Pooshipaw only appears at night – 'dark is for secrets', he malevolently explains to Simon – and always unbidden, uninvited. Its association with the tiger, albeit a toy one, allies it to notions of preying on the weak and defenceless. We are told that the Pooshipaw is a mere creature of his master, Bad Jack, made 'only for doing [his] master's dirty work'. The impression that the Pooshipaw is the personification of the phallus is underlined by Birdie's account of the intended invasion. 'The Pooshipaw takes the child away, do you see. It hollows it out, then takes it away and leaves it something else instead … a dead shell that looks like a child.' This is a description of both the act of violation and the loss of innocence which results in the death of childhood. *Dream Invader*, of course, is primarily about not the loss, but the restoration of childhood, and the prevention of the loss of innocence, preoccupations symptomatic of what Marina Warner (1994) calls our 'raging, yearning desire to work back to a pristine state of goodness'.

This desire to re-establish the Romantic concept of children as emblems of purity and perfection is intertwined with notions of the timeless, natural wisdom of Birdie, the ancient wise woman of the novel. She is a kind of Babayaga figure, described by Germaine Greer (1991) as 'a good witch, who is especially kind to children; she is also a rustic witch'.

In a sense this rural nurturing female refuses, in John Gillis's (2002) phrase, to 'propel them [children] too early into adulthood', an action that is at the very centre of the urban exploitative philosophy of Bad Jack. Whelan's particular focus on gender in this novel illustrates what Warner describes as 'the unease surrounding men', for 'alongside the warrior, the figure of the sex criminal has dug deep roots into the cultural formation of masculinity'.

Whelan's fiction emerges from a society which exhibits confusion and guilt in its relationship with children and with the concepts that surround childhood. We imbue the young with qualities of purity, virtue and vulnerability, qualities we as adults see ourselves as having lost. In Whelan's work the emergence of children into adult society is rarely joyous, rarely celebrated. While the two young protagonists in *Out of Nowhere* are amused and happy at their new status as young adults, this is intimately linked to the fact that they are Tellenes, and their future will be played out not in Ireland, nor on Earth, but on their home planet. Similarly, in *Dream Invader*, Saskia's adulthood, we are told, will be spent in Holland, 'the beach back home at the bottom of her Irish garden' being experienced only in dreams.

Whelan presents his readers with a vision of Ireland which is violent and exploitative, and ruled over by – as satirised in *Out of Nowhere* – besuited and ineffectual men whose actions are dictated by American imperialism. It is not a place for children, destroying as it does the positive outlook, trust and optimism which initially characterise Whelan's fictional young. Part of his solution is for us as a society to embrace the traditional wisdom, power, love and nurturing qualities of women such as Lily Conway, the 'buddha-like' Birdie, and the 'fat little woman with blue-rinsed hair' who dictates the future to world politicians before nonchalantly disappearing through the wall. This endorsement of the attributes of those too often ignored by society, mothers and old women, comes from an author who is described in an introductory biographical note in his first novel as a 'full-time father'. A case, perhaps, of the physician healing himself.

References

Gillis, John R (2002) 'Birth of the Virtual Child: Origins of Our Contradictory Images of Children' in Joseph Dunne and James Kelly (eds) *Childhood and its Discontents* Dublin: The Liffey Press

Greer, Germaine (1991) *The Change* London: Hamish Hamilton

Warner, Marina (1994) *Managing Monsters: Six Myths of our Time* London: Vintage

The Contributors

Valerie Coghlan, librarian at the Church of Ireland College of Education, also lectures in University College Dublin and St Patrick's College, Drumcondra and is co-editor of *Bookbird* and former co-editor of *Inis* and of two books about Irish children's books.

Robert Dunbar was formerly head of English at the Church of Ireland College of Education, Dublin. He writes and broadcasts regularly on children's literature and has edited, or co-edited, five books on the subject.

Lucinda Jacob is a children's writer/illustrator and a textile artist. She also writes poetry, TV and radio scripts and reviews for specialist magazines and leads creative workshops for schoolchildren.

Celia Keenan is a lecturer in English, director of the MA in Children's Literature, St Patrick's College, Drumcondra and president of ISSCL. She co-edited *Studies in Children's Literature 1500–2000* and *Treasure Islands: Studies in Children's Literature:*

Liz Morris is an English as an additional language teacher in a Dublin primary school. She co-edited *Cross-Currents: A Guide to Multicultural Books for Young People* and regularly co-edits CBI's recommended reading guide *Bookfest*.

Ciara Ní Bhroin lectures in English literature in Marino Institute of Education. She has published on the work of Lady Gregory, Eilís Dillon, Maria Edgeworth and Robert Cormier.

Lucy O' Dea works in a Dublin primary school. She served on the committee of CBI and on the board of IBBY Ireland. She co-edited *Changing*

Faces, Changing Places: A Guide to Multicultural Books for Children.

Siobhán Parkinson is a writer. Her best-known title is the Bisto-award-winning *Sisters ... No Way!* (O'Brien). She is writer-in-residence to the Marino Institute of Education and is co-editor of the international journal on children's literature, *Bookbird,* and former co-editor of *Inis.*

AJ Piesse is senior lecturer in English and Fellow of Trinity College Dublin. She works on early modern drama and on children's literature, especially Irish children's literature and (currently) older people in children's books.

Carole Redford lectures on the MA course in children's literature at St Patrick's College, Drumcondra. She has contributed essays on children's literature to a number of Irish, British and American publications.

John Short is a graduate of Edinburgh College of Art and the Royal College of Art in London. He is a senior lecturer in illustration and drawing in DIT in Dublin, and is a practising illustrator, portrait painter and artist.

Index